LEE CANTER'S

HOMEWORK WITHOUT TEARS FOR TEACHERS

Grades 1-3

A Publication of Lee Canter & Associates Inc.

Staff Writers
Ann de la Sota
Marcia Shank
Jim Thompson

Illustrators
Patty Briles
Bob McMahon

Editorial Staff
Marlene Canter
Barbara Shadlow
Kathy Winberry

Design
Tom Winberry
Bob Winberry

P.O. Box 2113, Santa Monica, CA 90406

ISBN 0-939007-19-3

Printed in the United States of America
First printing August 1988; Second printing February 1989

CONTENTS

Preface v

Chapter 1 Homework Without Tears 1

Chapter 2 Establishing a Homework Policy 5

Chapter 3 How to Teach Your Students to Do Homework Responsibly 13

Chapter 4 4 Steps to Giving Effective Homework Assignments 35

Chapter 5 How to Motivate Students to Do Their Homework 49

Chapter 6 What to Do If Students Do Not Complete Homework 56

Chapter 7 Creative Homework Models 65

Conclusion 77

Appendix 79

Recommended Reading 119

PREFACE

To establish the best possible environment for teaching and learning in school, we at Lee Canter & Associates have developed a complete behavior management system—for teachers, administrators, support staff and parents. Our program, Assertive Discipline, has made a dramatic difference, nationwide, in the education of children.

In working with teachers over the years to solve behavior problems in school, we saw one issue surface again and again: problems with homework. Recently, Gallup Poll statistics showed that the most frequently recurring problem in school is the subject of homework.

To succeed in school, students must be able to do homework, and do it well. In our Homework Without Tears program, we're dedicated to helping them do that. In *Homework Without Tears for Teachers,* we'll show you your part in the homework process, and just how you can help your students achieve success.

Chapter 1
HOMEWORK WITHOUT TEARS

With homework, more is not necessarily better. As a matter of fact, unless homework is effective, we'd be better off without it. Homework that causes frustration and tears is much worse than no homework at all.

Lee Canter

There are perhaps no more important homework assignments than those given to children during their early years. Their experience with those first assignments can influence their attitude toward homework for years to come. It is essential, then, that homework in the early grades results in success and good feelings rather than tears.

If you are reading this, you believe homework has value for your students and you care about making your assignments as effective as possible. You may believe, as many educators do, that homework can reinforce what you teach in the classroom, improve student performance, help students develop effective study habits and provide an important day-to-day link between home and school. Many researchers agree that effective homework may do all of this and more.

Homework and Students in Grades 1-3

In the early grades, homework is often used to extend the school day, with practice assignments to review and reinforce material covered in class. But there can be other valuable goals and purposes for assigning homework.

For one, homework can be used to foster independent study habits.

During the school day, you, the teacher, structure most of the students' activities. What is to be done and when it is to be completed is determined by you. Homework, on the other hand, is left to students (with the help of their parents) to schedule. This process leads to students' learning about following directions, working on their own, beginning and completing a task, managing their time and working to their full potential. These habits of effort and concentration will serve the students well as they progress toward later grades.

Homework in the early grades should be looked upon as building on successes. The process that a first-grader goes through of taking a worksheet home, completing it and bringing it back to school should be regarded as a major success. Completing a homework assignment appropriately at this age is an accomplishment to be recognized and rewarded.

In early grades developing basic homework habits is as important as the work itself. And good homework habits are fostered by praise and encouragement. Young children are going to forget or lose homework from time to time. But those times are of less importance than those when they do remember it. Your words of praise for remembered assignments are the best habit-forming tools at your disposal.

But even with all of the positive effects homework can have, it may also be an unpleasant experience for everyone involved.

If your students are frustrated because they can't succeed at homework, they will end up in tears. If parents are angry because homework means nightly battles with their children, they will be in tears. And if you find yourself buried beneath mounds of papers which you feel are meaningless, then you will be in tears.

Homework and You

Every time you give a homework assignment you are involving three groups of people in the homework process: your students, the parents and you. For homework to be effective, students have to remember to take it home, do it and bring it back; you must conscientiously assign work students are able to do; and parents must provide help and motivation at home.

When you think about it, homework asks for a lot from everyone involved. And you are the key. Homework starts and ends with you.

You are responsible for laying the groundwork for effective homework. You should:

- Teach students how to take assignments home, how to find a quiet place to work, how to do the work themselves, how to do their best work, and how to bring completed assignments back to school.
- Teach parents when and how to help their children, and how to reinforce good work habits.
- Assign work that your students are able to do, give clear directions, collect and check assignments and provide consistent positive reinforcement to both students and parents.

Yes, this is going to take time and effort on your part. But if you give homework, it is going to take your (and parents' and students') time and effort one way or another. *Homework Without Tears for Teachers* will help you make the time and effort spent as profitable as possible by giving everyone involved the skills they need.

Homework and Parents

In the early grades, homework provides a golden opportunity to involve parents in the education of their children in a positive way.

One thing researchers agree on is the importance of parents' interest and involvement to children's success in school. Parental motivation and support are the two most important factors in determining whether a child will do well in school.

It is important that you let parents know how much of an impact they can have on their children's achievement. With homework, parents have an opportunity to help their children succeed in school. The more parents provide positive support, the better their children will achieve.

What is *Homework Without Tears?*

Homework Without Tears for Teachers is a systematic approach to effective homework based both on research and on the experience of master teachers. *Homework Without Tears for Teachers* will give you the ideas, materials and skills you need for yourself, your students and their parents to ensure homework is done consistently and responsibly.

This book will show you:

How to establish a homework policy.

- Guidelines for developing an effective homework policy and for communicating that policy to students and parents.

How to teach your students to do homework.

- Seven lesson plans to teach students to do homework responsibly.
- Parent Tip Sheets to involve parents in each lesson.

How to assign effective homework.

- Guidelines for determining effective homework assignments.
- Teacher-tested tips for collecting and correcting homework.

How to motivate students to do their homework.

- How to motivate individual students to do homework.
- Motivational techniques for your entire class.

What to do when students do not complete homework.

- How to communicate with parents and get their support when children do not do homework.
- Techniques you can use at school when students do not complete homework.

How to assign more creative homework.

- Creative Homework Models that can be applied to all subject areas.

Homework Without Tears for Teachers will make the homework process a more rewarding experience for you, your students and their parents. But the first step must be yours and there's no better time to start than right now.

Chapter 2

ESTABLISHING A HOMEWORK POLICY

Teachers who have an effective approach to homework start by developing a homework policy. The policy establishes a foundation for homework by stating your expectations for everyone involved in the homework process.

A homework policy is particularly important in the early grades because of the necessary involvement on the part of the parents. Often too much or too little help from parents can present a problem. A homework policy that specifically describes both student and parent responsibilities is essential to ensure the effectiveness of your homework assignments.

Many schools or districts already have a homework policy in place for you to use. If there is no such policy, it is important that you establish one on your own or with the help of your fellow teachers and your administrator.

Ideally, homework policies should provide a schoolwide plan that gradually introduces homework and teaches study habits in early grades. However, if a schoolwide policy is not practical, it is recommended that you work with other teachers at your own grade level to achieve some degree of uniformity.

A homework policy should:

Give a rationale for homework.

You cannot assume that students or parents understand why homework is given or how important it is. Therefore, you should explain the benefits of homework and why you are going to give it. For instance, your rationale could include that homework is important because:

- It develops homework habits essential for succeeding in later grades.
- It provides practice time to reinforce skills and material learned in class.
- It teaches students to work independently.
- It provides a daily opportunity for parents to encourage their children to succeed in school.

Explain the types of homework you will assign.

It is important that both parents and students know that you are doing your part to ensure that all students have the ability to do the homework you assign.

Your policy should state that homework you assign:

- Will reinforce material already covered in class.
- Will require only those skills students have already learned in class.

Chapter 4, "4 Steps to Giving Effective Homework Assignments," will cover in detail the guidelines to assigning effective homework.

Inform parents of the amount and frequency of homework.

Research has shown that regular homework assignments produce more learning than less consistently assigned homework. Also, how you schedule homework is important in helping children develop homework habits. Random assignments make it difficult for children to get into the habit of doing homework. It is best, therefore, to select certain days on which you will regularly give homework.

For instance, Tuesday and Thursday might be your homework nights. Parents then know to check with children on these nights to see that assignments are brought home, completed and sent back to you.

If regular "homework nights" do not fit into your style of teaching, we suggest the use of a homework calendar (see page 64). You can use the calendar not only to note homework nights, but special days such as "show and tell" and library book return day. Also, by sending a calendar home you can encourage parents to help children check it daily so that they can begin managing their own time.

The amount of homework you assign will depend on your community, your district, your principal, your class, your teaching style and even the individual student. Research shows that 10 to 45 minutes of homework per night is a workable time range for students in first through third grades.

Of course, this is simply a guideline. The length of assignments *must always be determined by the individual needs and capabilities of the students involved.*

It is important, therefore, for you to include in your homework policy:

- The days on which you will usually assign homework.
- The amount of time it should take students to complete their homework.

Provide guidelines for when and how students are to complete homework.

For students to meet your expectations about completing homework, you must clearly define how you expect students to go about doing their assignments.

Typical expectations include that:

- All assignments will be completed.
- Students will turn in work that is neatly done.
- Students will turn in homework on time.

State that you will keep a record of assignments completed and not completed.

Your policy should state that you will keep a record of all homework assignments completed and not completed. The fact that you will check all homework is enough to motivate many students to do their homework. Also, this type of record keeping says something to both students and parents about the value you place on each and every assignment.

Let parents know how you will positively reinforce students who complete homework.

Your use of positive reinforcement is essential in motivating younger students to do homework. Your policy, therefore, should include:

- An explanation of the positives you will use for individual students: praise, awards, notes home to the parents.
- The positive rewards that can be earned by the entire class.

Chapter 5, "How to Motivate Students to Do Their Homework," will explain in detail how to use positive reinforcement to motivate students.

Explain how homework will affect students' grades.

Students and parents need to know if homework will be considered separately or as a percentage of a citizenship or a subject grade. Whatever system you or your school uses should be stated in your homework policy.

Clarify what is expected of the parent.

Since you do not follow the homework and the students home, it is up to parents to help see that homework is completed. Your homework policy needs to cover the specific type of support you expect from parents.

- **You should expect parents to establish homework as a priority for their children.**

  Parents must not allow other activities to adversely affect their children's homework. Some children may prefer going out to play for a while or having a snack before doing homework, and that is all right. But allowing children to put homework off until just before bedtime when they are too tired to do a good job is not acceptable.

- **You should expect parents to make sure that their children have a quiet place to work at home.**

  Children do not need a lot of space in which to do homework. The kitchen table or a corner of the living room is fine, as long as it is well lit and quiet during homework time.

- **You should expect parents to establish a Daily Homework Time.**

  The younger the children, the less specific Daily Homework Time needs to be. With a first-grader, "first thing after dinner" is specific enough. With older children, more scheduling is needed as other activities (sports, music lessons, etc.) start to fill up their afternoons and evenings.

- **You should expect parents to provide help to their children.**

  If children say that they do not understand a homework assignment, parents should help them read the directions. If they still have difficulty doing the work, parents may help them with the first part of the assignment. Parents should also be encouraged to work with children who need drill and practice in math, spelling or reading

  Other techniques for parents to use to help and encourage their children can be found in Chapters 5 and 6.

- **You should expect parents to provide positive support when homework is completed.**

  Children of any age cannot receive too much praise and support from parents. Ideally, parents should praise some aspect of every one of their child's homework assignments.

- **You should expect parents to contact you if children have problems with homework.**

  Parents need to let you know when problems with homework arise. This can be done simply by writing you a note on, or attaching it to, homework.

Explain what you will do when students do not complete homework.

When students continually do not complete homework assignments, your homework policy should provide that:

- You will contact parents to discuss the problem and provide them with resources they can use to help their children get homework done. (See Chapter 6.)
- If you do not get support from parents or if that support is not working, then you will need to take further steps with the student at school, such as requesting that parents sign completed homework every night, or having the student miss recess or lunch to complete homework.

It is important to note here that in some instances students may be prevented from doing homework by circumstances outside of their control. You must be sensitive to your own students' situations at home and be prepared to help students find solutions should this type of problem arise.

How to Use the Homework Policy

If you have developed your own homework policy, give a copy to your administrator for approval. Some administrators may require that they have a copy of your homework policy on file. In any case, it is a good idea to share your policy with your administrator in case parents contact him or her with questions or problems. Your efforts can't be supported unless your administrator knows what your policy is.

Discuss the homework policy with students.

At the beginning of the school year or whenever you begin the Homework Without Tears program, present your homework policy to your students and have a discussion regarding the guidelines. Make sure that you allow enough time to answer all of the students' questions.

Send the homework policy home to parents.

Send a copy of your homework policy home to parents. It is important that all parents understand exactly what you expect of them and their children in the homework process. With the policy, send a letter home instructing the parents to discuss the policy with their children. Provide a tear-off section on the accompanying letter for both parents and the student to sign acknowledging that they have read and discussed the homework policy. Then have the student bring the signed portion of the letter back to you.

Summary

Establishing your homework policy is the first step toward effective homework. It helps you clarify your goals for what you want to accomplish with your homework assignments. It helps you identify your expectations for everyone involved in the homework process and provides the means of communicating those expectations to both students and parents.

SAMPLE HOMEWORK POLICY

Second Grade

Dear Parent,

I will be assigning homework because I believe it is important that students begin to develop good homework habits in early grades. Also, homework gives me a way of having students practice what I have taught in class.

I will assign homework Tuesday and Thursday nights. Homework should take students from 15 minutes to 1/2 hour to complete each night.

I expect the students to do the work on their own and ask for help only after they have given it their best effort. Homework will cover only material that students have already been taught in class.

To help their children do their best with homework, I will ask that parents help them find a quiet place to work at home, help them decide on the best time of day to do homework assignments and make doing homework a priority at home.

If children have trouble with an assignment, I ask that parents check to see that they understand the directions. If children still have difficulty, parents may help them with the first part of the assignment. If children still cannot complete a homework assignment, I ask that parents do not do the work for their children and request that they write me a note explaining what they believe to be the problem.

I will encourage parents to praise their children's work each night. I believe parents' words of support are the single most important way to motivate children to do well in school.

I will check all homework. I also believe in the value my positive support plays in motivating children to develop good study habits. I will give students praise and other incentives when they do their homework properly. Homework assignments will comprise 25% of students' citizenship grade.

If children do not complete homework on a regular basis, I will contact the parents. It is important that parents and I work together to make sure their children develop the study habits that will be needed in later grades.

If there is a legitimate reason why students are not able to finish homework, I ask that parents send a note to me on the day the homework is due stating the reason it was not completed.

Teacher Signature

Chapter 3

HOW TO TEACH YOUR STUDENTS TO DO HOMEWORK RESPONSIBLY

Many students have difficulty with homework simply because they lack proper study habits. They forget to bring assignments back to class, they study in front of the television set or while talking on the phone, and they always seem to have time in their busy schedules for everything but homework.

This chapter gives you a series of lessons that will teach your students—and their parents—how to do homework responsibly. The assignments contained in the lessons are designed to be the first homework assignments the students receive. If possible, the lessons should be presented in the first week or two of school. What the student learns from these lessons can then be applied to homework assignments the rest of the year.

To be most effective, these lessons must be presented before any academic homework is assigned.

The Following Lessons Are Included In This Chapter:

Lesson 1:	Introducing the Homework Policy
Lesson 2:	Returning Homework to School On Time
Lesson 3:	Setting Up a Study Area at Home
Lesson 4:	Creating a Homework Survival Kit
Lesson 5:	Planning Daily Homework Time
Lesson 6:	Doing Homework on Your Own
Lesson 7:	Rewarding Yourself for Homework Success

Each lesson includes the following components:

A **Teacher's Lesson Plan** outlining the rationale, objective and procedure for the lesson. The lesson plans are contained within this chapter.

A **Student Worksheet** to reinforce and expand the lesson. Student Worksheet reproducible masters are in the Appendix section of this book.

A **Parent Tip Sheet** designed to keep parents informed of specific ways they can help their children do homework successfully. Reproducible masters are in the Appendix. (Note: There is no Parent Tip Sheet for Lesson 1.)

To use the lessons in this chapter most effectively, first determine a time frame in which you will teach the lessons.

Note: All of the lessons need to be taught together in the space of one or two weeks.

Follow this sequence when presenting each lesson:

- Read the lesson plan to familiarize yourself with the rationale, objectives and activities for the lesson.
- Make one copy for each student of the Student Worksheets and Parent Tip Sheet for the lesson.
- Teach the lesson to your students:
  - Introduce the concept.
  - Discuss the concept with your students.
  - Explain the homework assignment and distribute the Student Worksheets.
  - Distribute and discuss the Parent Tip Sheets.
  - Have students take home their worksheets and Parent Tip Sheets.
- Follow up as indicated on the lesson plan.

You are now ready to begin teaching your students to do their homework responsibly. Proceed to Lesson 1 on the next page.

Lesson 1

INTRODUCING THE HOMEWORK POLICY

RATIONALE

A homework policy establishes a firm foundation for homework by stating the expectations and responsibilities of everyone involved in the homework process—teacher, students and parents. In Lesson 1, students will be introduced to your homework policy and learn exactly what is expected of them regarding homework.

OBJECTIVE

After being introduced to the homework policy in class, the students will take home a copy of the policy, discuss it with their parents, obtain appropriate signatures, and return signatures to school.

MATERIALS

Homework Policy, Letter to parents

PROCEDURE

INTRODUCE THE IMPORTANCE OF EVERYONE—TEACHER, PARENT AND STUDENT—BEING INVOLVED IN HOMEWORK

1 Tell students that homework involves more than just the student. Explain that homework is a responsibility that involves the teacher, the students *and* their parents.

2 Ask students to tell what they think their own homework responsibilities might be. List their ideas on the board.

Examples:

- Remembering to take homework assignments home.
- Remembering to do the assignment.
- Remembering to bring homework back to school.
- Doing the work neatly.
- Trying to do the homework on your own.

3 Explain to students that during the next few days you will be teaching them some special skills that will help them do their homework assignments more responsibly.

4 Now ask students to talk about what their parents' homework responsibilities might be. List their ideas on the board.

Examples:

- Making sure the student has a place to study at home.
- Reminding the student to do homework.
- Making sure that necessary homework supplies are available.
- Helping the student get to the library when necessary.
- Reading and checking homework assignments.

5 Tell students that it is important for parents, too, to learn about better ways of doing homework—and what they can do to help their children. Explain that during the next few days you will be sending Parent Tip Sheets home that will give their parents lots of information about helping with homework.

Note: Before you introduce the homework policy, make sure that students understand what homework is and why you are going to be giving them homework assignments. For example, explain to students that one reason for doing homework is to practice skills learned in class. Show (or talk about) the kinds of assignments they will be doing.

DISCUSS HOW A HOMEWORK POLICY WILL HELP EVERYONE—TEACHER, STUDENT AND PARENTS—UNDERSTAND AND FULFILL THEIR RESPONSIBILITIES

1 Tell students that tonight you are going to give each of them a written homework policy to take home. Explain that a homework policy is a list of standards that will help students and parents understand their homework responsibilities. Read the policy standards to the class.

2 Explain why a homework policy is needed. (So that parents and students alike will clearly understand your expectations about homework.)

3 Tell about the positives you will use when homework is done appropriately. Explain the consequences that will be imposed when homework is not done.

4 Check for student understanding by having them paraphrase each of the standards you read.

5 Give each child a signed (by you) copy of the homework policy and a cover letter to take home to parents.

SAMPLE HOMEWORK POLICY

Second Grade

Dear Parent,

I will be assigning homework because I believe it is important that students begin to develop good homework habits in early grades. Also, homework gives me a way of having students practice what I have taught in class.

I will assign homework Tuesday and Thursday nights. Homework should take students from 15 minutes to 1/2 hour to complete each night.

I expect the students to do the work on their own and ask for help only after they have given it their best effort. Homework will cover only material that students have already been taught in class.

To help their children do their best with homework, I will ask that parents help them find a quiet place to work at home, help them decide on the best time of day to do homework assignments and make doing homework a priority at home.

If children have trouble with an assignment, I ask that parents check to see that they understand the directions. If children still have difficulty, parents may help them with the first part of the assignment. If children still cannot complete a homework assignment, I ask that parents do not do the work for their children and request that they write me a note explaining what they believe to be the problem.

I will encourage parents to praise their children's work each night. I believe parents' words of support are the single most important way to motivate children to do well in school.

I will check all homework. I also believe in the value my positive support plays in motivating children to develop good study habits. I will give students praise and other incentives when they do their homework properly. Homework assignments will comprise 25% of students' citizenship grade.

If children do not complete homework on a regular basis, I will contact the parents. It is important that parents and I work together to make sure their children develop the study habits that will be needed in later grades.

If there is a legitimate reason why students are not able to finish homework, I ask that parents send a note to me on the day the homework is due stating the reason it was not completed.

Teacher Signature

EXPLAIN THE HOMEWORK ASSIGNMENT: TAKE THE HOMEWORK POLICY HOME, READ IT WITH PARENTS, AND RETURN THE SIGNATURE PORTION TO SCHOOL

1 Explain to students that they are to read the homework policy with their parents that night. Tell them that after reading the policy together, you want the students *and* their parents to sign the accompanying letter in the appropriate spaces. (Show the signature portion of the letter.) Explain that their signatures will let you know that parents and students understand what is expected of everyone regarding homework.

2 Tell students that you want them to return the signatures to school the next day.

FOLLOW UP

1 NEXT DAY Collect signed papers. Review the homework policy once more to make certain that all students understand their responsibilities.

2 Review your homework rules on a regular basis throughout the year.

3 Do your part in enforcing the homework policy by always following through with your positives and consequences. Be consistent. Let your students know that in your class homework *is* important.

Lesson 2

RETURNING HOMEWORK TO SCHOOL ON TIME

RATIONALE

Remembering to bring homework assignments back to school when they are due is an important responsibility a student must develop. Lesson 2 provides students with skills that will help them develop the habit of returning homework to school on time.

OBJECTIVE

Students will choose a spot at home where they will put completed homework assignments each night. They will mark this spot with a "Homework Drop Spot" sign. Consistent use of this Homework Drop Spot will help develop the habit of always putting finished homework in the same place each night—thus making it easier to remember to bring it back to school.

MATERIALS

Student Worksheet 2 (Appendix page 83)
Parent Tip Sheet 2 (Appendix page 97)

PROCEDURE

INTRODUCE THE CONCEPT OF REMEMBERING TO BRING HOMEWORK BACK TO SCHOOL EACH DAY

Students who have previously received homework assignments:

1 Ask students to think about times they have forgotten to bring homework assignments back to school. Have them give reasons why they forgot (e.g., couldn't find it, were too rushed to remember, lost it).

2 Ask what happens at home on mornings when they can't find their homework. How do they feel? How do their parents feel? How do students feel back in class when they've done the homework assignment and left it at home?

3 Have students brainstorm ideas that might help them remember to bring homework assignments back to school each day.

Students who have had no previous experience with homework:

1 Ask students to think about times they forgot to bring something home, or forgot to take something with them.

Examples:

- Forgot to bring a jacket home from school.
- Forgot to take a toy home from a friend's house.
- Forgot to take a toothbrush on an overnight.

2 Ask students why they think they sometimes forget these things (e.g. , they get too rushed, they are too busy to remember, something distracts them, no one reminded them).

3 Explain to students that an important part of learning to do homework responsibly is learning to remember to bring the finished homework back to school the next day. Tell students that remembering to bring homework back to school is going to be *their* job. It's not up to Mom or Dad to remind them. Homework is *their* responsibility.

4 Have students brainstorm ideas that might help them remember to bring homework assignments back to school each day (e.g., put it in their backpack, leave a note on the refrigerator, put it in the car, etc.).

DISCUSS WAYS OF HELPING STUDENTS REMEMBER TO BRING HOMEWORK BACK TO SCHOOL

1 Tell students that you want to introduce an idea that will help them bring homework back to school on time.

2 Discuss with students the importance of getting into the habit of putting their completed homework in the same place each night. (Explain that a habit is something that you do so often or for such a long time that you do it without thinking.) Ask the students to share their ideas for special "Homework Drop Spots" where homework goes as soon as it is completed and where it is easy to "spot" on the way out the door in the morning. (Example: Assignment first goes into a notebook, then in backpack, then in a spot by the door.)

3 Point out that if they consistently put homework in the same place each night, it will soon become a habit to do so.

EXPLAIN THE HOMEWORK ASSIGNMENT (WORKSHEET 2)

1 Tell students that you are giving them an assignment that will help them remember to bring homework back to school. Ask students to once again tell you what a Homework Drop Spot is. Then explain that their homework that night will be to color a Homework Drop Spot sign and to select a Homework Drop Spot at home.

2 Show Worksheet 2: X Marks the Homework Drop Spot. Tell students that they are to color the cartoon X on the worksheet. Point out that the X stands for "X Marks the Homework Drop Spot." They are to tape the worksheet on the Homework Drop Spot they have chosen.

3 Remind students that as soon as they finish their homework each night it is to be put at the Homework Drop Spot. If they remember to do this over and over again it will soon become a habit, and forgetting to bring homework back to school won't be a problem!

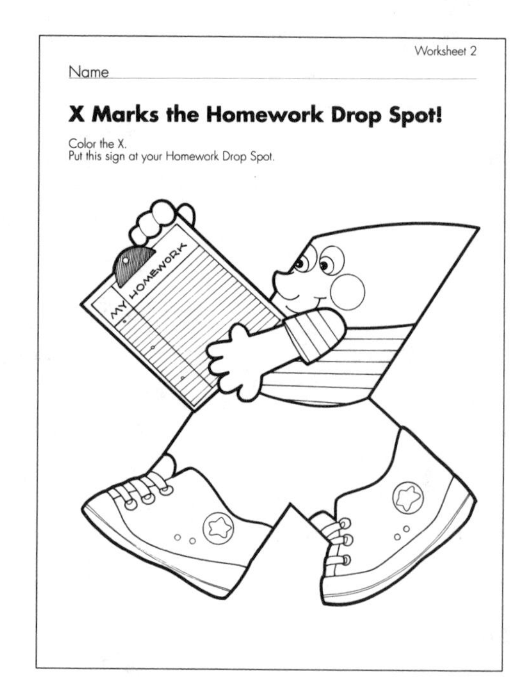
Worksheet 2

Name

X Marks the Homework Drop Spot!

Color the X.
Put this sign at your Homework Drop Spot.

SHOW PARENT TIP SHEET 2

1. Encourage students to compare and talk about what's happening in the two cartoons.
2. Explain that the Parent Tip Sheet will give their parents information about helping the students choose a Homework Drop Spot at home.
3. Read the Parent Tips to them as appropriate.
4. Make sure students take the Parent Tip Sheet home.

Parent Tip Sheet 2

CHOOSE A HOMEWORK DROP SPOT

HOMEWORK WITH TEARS

In the early grades, your child must begin to develop the study habits that will be the foundation of his or her success in school in the years to come. Remembering to bring homework assignments back to school is one of the most important habits your child must develop.

Choosing a special Homework Drop Spot at home will help your child develop the habit of always putting completed assignments in the same place each night.

PRAISE

HOMEWORK WITHOUT TEARS

Agree on the Homework Drop Spot your child chooses. Make sure it is in a location that is convenient for you, too.

Help your child choose a Homework Drop Spot that's easy to "spot" on the way out the door in the morning.

Respect the Homework Drop Spot. Don't let other things clutter or cover it.

FOLLOW UP

1. Ask a few students each day to share how their Homework Drop Spots are working so they can evaluate whether they need to make any changes, and so others can hear what works and what doesn't work.
2. Remember that the goal of this activity is to form a habit that the students will benefit from for the rest of the year. Be consistent in rewarding students when they bring homework assignments back on time.

Lesson 3

SETTING UP A STUDY AREA

RATIONALE

Students—and their parents—must understand that to do homework successfully, they must have a place in which to work. The study area must be well lit, quiet, and have all necessary supplies at hand. Lesson 3 will give students the skills and motivation they need to set up a proper study area at home.

OBJECTIVE

With the help of their parents, students will choose a study area at home. They will then color, cut and paste pictures to show how their personal study areas look.

MATERIALS

Student Worksheet 3a (Appendix page 84), Student Worksheet 3b (Appendix page 85), "Do Not Disturb" sign (Appendix page 86), Parent Tip Sheet 3 (Appendix page 98)

PROCEDURE

INTRODUCE THE CONCEPT OF DOING HOMEWORK IN A STUDY AREA

1 Have individual students talk about where they have done homework assignments in the past. (If this is their first experience with homework, ask them to talk about quiet places at home where they like to look at books or draw.) Was this a good place to do homework? What, if any, were some of the problems they had working in this location? What did they like about the location?

2 Share ideas about the following questions:

Should they do homework in a noisy room? Why or why not?

Should they do homework in front of a TV? Why or why not?

Should they do homework while they are eating? Why or why not?

Should they do homework outside while they are playing? Why or why not?

3 Ask students to talk about what they think a good study area should be like. Make sure that the following points are included: A good study area is one that is well lit, quiet, and has all necessary supplies at hand.

DISCUSS SETTING UP A PERSONAL STUDY AREA AT HOME

1 Encourage all students to think about locations in their own homes that might be good for studying. Share ideas. Ask students to tell why the location would be a good place for doing homework.

2 Make it clear to students that even if they usually do most of their homework after school in another location, such as the library, at a babysitter's, or at an after-school care program, they *still* need a place at home where they can study at other times.

3 Emphasize that their study area can be in any part of the home: kitchen, bedroom, living room, den, etc. It doesn't matter where it is as long as it's a place where the student can concentrate and get his or her work done.

4 Talk about the importance of making their personal study area a place they like to be while studying.

a. Have the students name things that they would *need* in a study area (a desk or table, a light, a chair).

b. Have each student name one special thing that he or she would *want* to add to the study area to make it more enjoyable and special (a comfortable pillow, a favorite stuffed animal, etc.).

Note: Recognize that some of your students may have real difficulty finding a quiet place to study at home. They may live in an overcrowded apartment, the environment may be unstable or chaotic, their parents may be unresponsive to their study needs, etc. Help these students explore study area alternatives. Talk about what they can do to help themselves by taking action on their own.

Some suggestions:

1 Find another place to do homework, such as the library or a friend's house.

2 Consistently ask their parents to support their study efforts by keeping sisters and brothers quiet during homework time.

3 Ask parents if one room can be off limits to others in the family during homework time.

4 Arrange with a brother or sister to do homework at the same time.

Be sure to ask students to give suggestions of their own to this problem.

EXPLAIN THE HOMEWORK ASSIGNMENT (WORKSHEETS 3A AND 3B)

1 Tell students that, *with their parents' help*, they are to choose a study area at home. Make it clear to students that this does not mean they need a special room of their own, only that there is some quiet place in the home where they can study. Explain that the homework assignment that night will be to color, cut and paste a picture of the study area that they have chosen.

2 Show Worksheet 3a: Study Area Cut-Outs. Tell students that this worksheet shows pictures of lots of things that might be in a study area. They are to color and cut out only the pictures of things that are in the study area they have chosen at their own home.

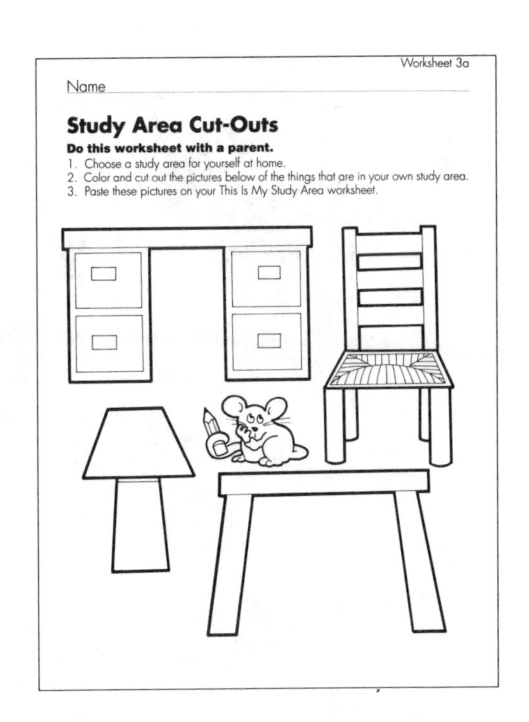
Worksheet 3a

Name

Study Area Cut-Outs

Do this worksheet with a parent.

1. Choose a study area for yourself at home.
2. Color and cut out the pictures below of the things that are in your own study area.
3. Paste these pictures on your This Is My Study Area worksheet.

3 Show Worksheet 3b: This Is My Study Area. Tell students that they are to paste their study area cut-outs on this worksheet. They are to make the picture look as much like their real study area as they can. Encourage students to draw additional things in the picture to make it look even more like their own home. Depending upon the study area they have chosen, these additional pictures could include curtains, doors, windows, a refrigerator, a bed, etc.

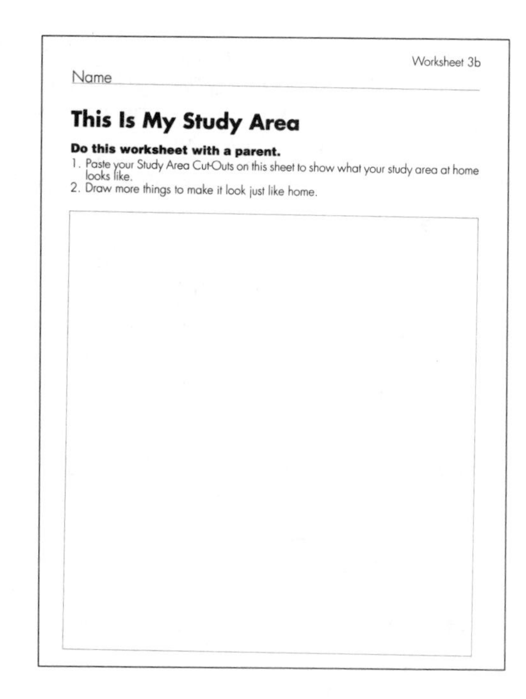

Worksheet 3b

Name

This Is My Study Area

Do this worksheet with a parent.

1. Paste your Study Area Cut-Outs on this sheet to show what your study area at home looks like.
2. Draw more things to make it look just like home.

SHOW PARENT TIP SHEET 3

1 Encourage students to compare and talk about what's happening in the cartoons.

2 Explain that the Parent Tip Sheet will give their parents information about helping them set up their own study areas.

3 Read the Parent Tips to them as appropriate.

4 Make sure that students take the Parent Tip Sheet home.

Parent Tip Sheet 3

CHOOSE A STUDY AREA AT HOME

HOMEWORK WITH TEARS

To do homework successfully, your child must have a place in which to work. The study area must be well lit, quiet, and have all necessary supplies.

Keep the radio and TV off while homework is being done.

Whenever possible, keep the study area off limits to brothers and sisters during homework time.

PRAISE your child when he or she does homework in the study area.

HOMEWORK WITHOUT TEARS

Help your child choose a location at home in which homework will be done. Even if your child does most of the homework at another location after school, there still should be a place in the home in which he or she can study.

Remember that your child does not need a lot of space in which to do homework. The kitchen table or a corner of the living room is fine, as long as it is well lit and quiet during homework time.

FOLLOW UP

1 Ask students to discuss how their study areas are working out for them.

2 Have students color the Do Not Disturb sign (Appendix page 86). Tell them to hang it in their study area at home.

3 As a related art project, have the students decorate cans or jars to be used as special pencil or crayon holders at home. They can also cover various shaped boxes to be used as desktop organizers.

Lesson 4

CREATING A HOMEWORK SURVIVAL KIT

RATIONALE

To complete homework assignments effectively, students must have available at home a collection of basic supplies. A Homework Survival Kit—containing the supplies needed to do homework—will help students get their homework done appropriately, and on time. Lesson 4 will give students the skills they need to create a Homework Survival Kit.

OBJECTIVE

Students will create a cut-and-paste Homework Survival Kit. They will apply the information learned in this activity to the creation of their own real Homework Survival Kits.

MATERIALS

Student Worksheet 4a (Appendix page 87), Student Worksheet 4b (Appendix page 88), Parent Tip Sheet 4 (Appendix page 99)

PROCEDURE

INTRODUCE THE CONCEPT OF CREATING A HOMEWORK SURVIVAL KIT

1 Tell students that an important part of getting homework assignments done is having all the supplies they need available in their study area.

2 Ask students to talk about what happens at home when they can't find something they must have in order to complete an assignment. (Example: They are to glue a picture on a piece of paper and they can't find the glue.)

3 Tell students that one way to solve this problem is by creating their own Homework Survival Kits. Explain that a Homework Survival Kit is a collection of all the materials they may need at one time or another to do their homework.

DISCUSS THE KINDS OF MATERIALS THAT SHOULD GO INTO A HOMEWORK SURVIVAL KIT AND DIFFERENT WAYS TO KEEP THESE MATERIALS ORGANIZED IN ONE PLACE AT HOME

1 Ask students to suggest items that they would include in a Homework Survival Kit. (See Suggested Materials list on the next page.) For each suggestion, have students tell how it would help in getting different kinds of homework done.

2 Play ***Homework Survival Kit Scavenger Hunt***

a. Place a variety of Homework Survival Kit materials around the classroom (at least two each of the items listed).

b. Tell students that they are each to find one item that should be part of a Homework Survival Kit.

c. Dismiss students for a one-minute search. When everyone has found an item, bring the class back together.

d. Let each student share his or her "find" and tell how that item might be used for doing homework.

SUGGESTED MATERIALS FOR A HOMEWORK SURVIVAL KIT

crayons ○ pencils ○ markers ○ sharpener ○ erasers glue or paste ○ tape ○ writing paper ○ construction paper ○ ruler ○ stapler ○ scissors ○ children's dictionary ○ paper clips

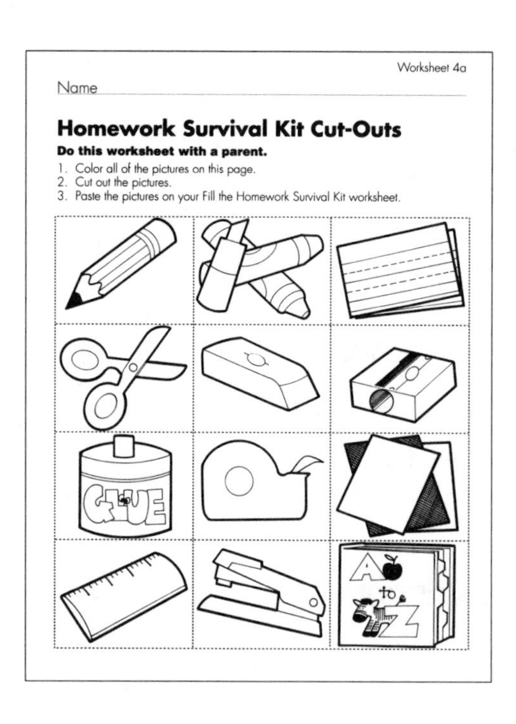

Worksheet 4a

Name

Homework Survival Kit Cut-Outs

Do this worksheet with a parent.

1. Color all of the pictures on this page.
2. Cut out the pictures.
3. Paste the pictures on your Fill the Homework Survival Kit worksheet.

3 Talk about some of the different ways students can keep all Homework Survival Kit materials in one place at home.

a. Put all the sample materials the students have gathered in the scavenger hunt into a shoebox or other container.

b. Ask students to suggest other types of containers that could be used (basket, lunchbox, desk drawer, etc.). Talk about advantages and disadvantages of each.

4 Suggest to students that if they usually do their homework in a location other than home, it might be a good idea to keep their Homework Survival Kit in that place.

EXPLAIN THE HOMEWORK ASSIGNMENT (WORKSHEETS 4A AND 4B)

1 Tell students that you are giving them an assignment that will help them organize and put together their own real Homework Survival Kits at home. Explain that their homework assignment that night will be to make a cut-and-paste Homework Survival Kit.

2 Show Worksheet 4a: Homework Survival Kit Cut-Outs. Tell students that this worksheet shows pictures of things that should be in a Homework Survival Kit. They are to color these pictures and cut them out.

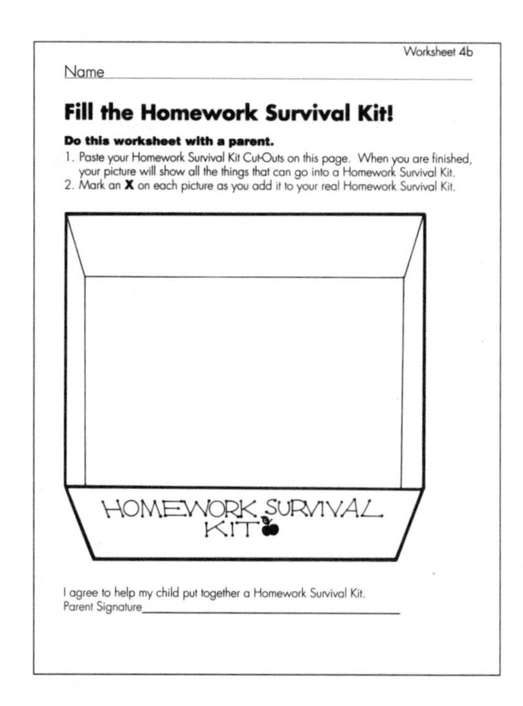

Worksheet 4b

Name

Fill the Homework Survival Kit!

Do this worksheet with a parent.

1. Paste your Homework Survival Kit Cut-Outs on this page. When you are finished, your picture will show all the things that can go into a Homework Survival Kit.
2. Mark an **X** on each picture as you add it to your real Homework Survival Kit.

HOMEWORK SURVIVAL KIT

I agree to help my child put together a Homework Survival Kit.
Parent Signature________________

3 Show Worksheet 4b: Fill the Homework Survival Kit. Tell students that they are to paste their cut-out pictures on this sheet to "Fill the Homework Survival Kit." Explain that they are then to have their parents sign the finished worksheet and are to return it to school the next day. Tell students that their parent's signature on this worksheet means that they agree to help the student put together his or her own real Homework Survival Kit.

4 Emphasize to students that their parents are not expected to run out and buy everything on the list. Explain that a complete Homework Survival Kit is a goal, something to work at building up.

5 Remind students to put their completed homework assignment in the Homework Drop Spot!

Note: If some of your students do not have the means to obtain materials for a Homework Survival Kit, you can help by allowing them to take "portable" Survival Kits home from school. Let students take home specific materials they will need to complete a homework assignment (glue, scissors, paper, etc.). Have them carry these materials back and forth from home. You might also check into the availability of supplies from school that could be given to students for the purpose of helping with homework. Keep in mind also that Homework Survival Kit items make excellent classroom rewards.

SHOW PARENT TIP SHEET 4

Parent Tip Sheet 4

CREATE A HOMEWORK SURVIVAL KIT

One of the keys to getting homework done is having supplies in one place. A Homework Survival Kit—containing supplies needed to do homework—will prevent your child from being continually distracted by the need to go searching for supplies, and will free you from last-minute trips to the store for paper, tape, glue, etc.

If your child does homework at a location other than home (such as the library or an after-school care program) make sure that his or her homework supplies are available there.

Respect your child's Homework Survival Kit. Don't use these supplies for other family needs.

AGREE

Give Homework Survival Kit materials as gifts. A dictionary, for example, is a special present that a child will use over and over again.

These are the supplies needed for a Homework Survival Kit:
*pencils • *writing paper • *crayons
markers • ruler • sharpener
erasers • glue or paste • tape
construction paper • stapler
scissors • paper clips • children's dictionary

* These are the most important supplies your child needs. Try to obtain these items as soon as possible. Add additional homework supplies as you are able to.

You don't need to gather all the materials in one day, but don't wait too long. Your child needs these supplies to do his or her best job on homework.

1. Encourage students to compare and talk about what's happening in the cartoons.
2. Explain that the Parent Tip Sheet will give their parents information about helping students create their own Homework Survival Kits at home.
3. Read the Parent Tips to them as appropriate.
4. Make sure students take the Parent Tip Sheet home.

FOLLOW UP

1. NEXT DAY Collect the cut-and-paste Homework Survival Kit worksheets and check for parent signatures. Return the worksheets to the students. Tell them to use the worksheet to help collect materials for their own Homework Survival Kits. Every time they add something to their Survival Kit, they should mark an X through that item on their cut-and-paste picture.
2. As a related art project, have the students decorate a small box that they can take home to use in the Homework Survival Kit in which to keep paper clips, crayons, pencils, etc.

Lesson 5

PLANNING DAILY HOMEWORK TIME

RATIONALE

Homework—like other activities and responsibilities—must be scheduled into a student's life. Lesson 5 will help students determine the best time for them to do homework.

OBJECTIVE

Students, with a parent's help, will record their after-school activities on a cut-and-paste worksheet. In doing so, they will determine when Daily Homework Time will be scheduled.

MATERIALS

Student Worksheet 5a (Appendix page 89), Student Worksheet 5b (Appendix page 90), Parent Tip Sheet 5 (Appendix page 100)

PROCEDURE

INTRODUCE THE CONCEPT OF DOING ACTIVITIES AT A CERTAIN TIME EACH DAY

1 Tell students that many of our regular activities are done at the same time each day.

Give students some introductory examples, then ask for them to give examples of their own.

Examples:

- Getting up in the morning.
- Eating breakfast.
- Going to school.
- Recess at school.
- Eating lunch.
- Getting out of school.
- Going home after school.
- Going to a babysitter after school.
- Eating dinner.
- Feeding the dog.
- Watching TV.
- Taking a bath.
- Brushing teeth.
- Going to bed.

2 Ask students to talk about why it is helpful to do things at the same time each day.

3 Tell students that homework is another activity which should be done at the same time each day. This special time can be called Daily Homework Time.

DISCUSS HOW DAILY HOMEWORK TIME CAN HELP GET HOMEWORK DONE

1. Ask students to think about some of the homework assignments they were given the previous year. Ask if they remember when they usually did their homework? (Note: These questions are applicable only to students who have previously received homework assignments. If homework is a new experience for your students, move on to discussion items 2 and 3 below.) Did they do it right after school? Later at night? On the school bus? Did they have any rules at home about when they were supposed to do their homework? Share comments.
2. Explain again that Daily Homework Time is a special time set aside just for homework. Tell students that when they have a Daily Homework Time, they will know every day exactly when it is time to sit down and get homework done. Ask students to tell why Daily Homework Time might help them get their homework done.
3. Ask students to tell when they think would be a good time for them to do their homework: right after school, after dinner, just before dinner, when Mom or Dad gets home.

EXPLAIN THE HOMEWORK ASSIGNMENT (WORKSHEETS 5A AND 5B)

1. Tell students that you are giving them an assignment that will help them decide and remember when they will do homework each day. *Explain that this assignment must be done with a parent's help.*
2. Show Worksheet 5a: After-School Activities Squares

   Point out the four squares on the page. Tell students that these squares show things that they probably do most days after school before they go to bed at night. Read the activities: Do homework; Play; Go home; Eat dinner. Explain to students that they are to cut out the four squares on this page and use them on another worksheet.

Name

After-School Activities Squares

Do this worksheet with a parent.

1. The pictures on this page show four things you do after school.
2. Cut out the pictures.
3. Paste them on your My Daily Schedule worksheet.

3 Show Worksheet 5b: My Daily Schedule.

Point out that this worksheet shows *other* activities students do each day. Read the following sequence: Go to school; Eat lunch; Go to recess; Get out of school. Explain to students that they usually do all of these activities at the same time each day. Remind them that they should also do homework at the same time each day. Now show the blank spaces on the worksheet. Tell students that they are to paste their cut-out squares in these spaces and number them in order. (Read the Activities Squares once more.) Tell them that they must paste these pictures in the order that they really do them. For example, do they do homework before they play? Do they do homework after dinner? Do they do homework before they go home (at an after-school care program or at a babysitter's)? Tell students that the reason they are doing this assignment is to help them choose a time when they will try to do homework each day. For that reason, they must do this assignment with a parent .

4 Tell students that there is a place on the worksheet for a parent's signature. They are to have a parent sign the completed worksheet and bring it back to school.

Name

Worksheet 5b

My Daily Schedule

Do this worksheet with a parent.

Parent Signature________________

1. Look at the pictures. Read the words.
2. Think about what you do after school.
3. Paste your After-School Activities Squares in order on numbers 5, 6, 7, and 8 .

(1) I go to school.	(2) I go to recess.	(3) I eat my lunch.	(4) I get out of school.
(5) What do you do right after school? PASTE HERE	(6) What do you do next? PASTE HERE	(7) What happens next? PASTE HERE	(8) What do you do after that? PASTE HERE

SHOW PARENT TIP SHEET 5

1 Encourage students to compare and talk about what's happening in the cartoons.

2 Explain that the Parent Tip Sheet will give their parents information about helping them set up Daily Homework Time.

3 Read them the Parent Tips if appropriate.

4 Make sure students take home the Parent Tip Sheet.

FOLLOW UP

1 NEXT DAY Check to see that students have completed their My Daily Schedule worksheets. Tell them to take the worksheets home again and put them on the refrigerator or in their study area. Encourage students to stick to a regular Daily Homework Time.

Parent Tip Sheet 5

SCHEDULE DAILY HOMEWORK TIME

HOMEWORK WITH TEARS

Help your child develop good homework habits by encouraging him or her to start homework at the same time each day. By scheduling Daily Homework Time, you will not only help your child get work done on time, but you will also ensure that homework is done at a time when you are available to assist your child.

Post your child's completed My Daily Schedule cut-and-paste activity on the refrigerator.

It is your responsibility to schedule Daily Homework Time for your child. For young children, the best time is often as soon as they (and you) arrive home at the end of the day.

Encourage your child to do homework during Daily Homework Time by giving lots of **PRAISE** each time homework is done appropriately.

HOMEWORK WITHOUT TEARS

Remind your child each day when he or she is to do homework.

Select a time when you or another responsible adult will be available to assist your child.

Try to schedule the same Daily Homework Time for all of your children. (This will make it more convenient for you to be available.)

Lesson 6

DOING HOMEWORK ON YOUR OWN

RATIONALE

Doing homework independently teaches a student responsibility and builds confidence and self-esteem. In Lesson 6 students will be encouraged to take pride in doing homework assignments on their own.

OBJECTIVE

Students will color and cut out "I Did It" squares, which are to be taped to any assignment that they "did on their own." They will continue to use these squares to identify assignments they are particularly proud of having done.

MATERIALS

Student Worksheet 6 (Appendix page 91)
Parent Tip Sheet 6 (Appendix page 101)

PROCEDURE

INTRODUCE THE IDEA THAT AS THEY GROW OLDER, STUDENTS ARE BEGINNING TO DO MORE AND MORE THINGS ON THEIR OWN

1 Ask students to talk about why it's important to learn to do more and more things on their own. Ask how they feel when they do something that they couldn't do on their own before.

2 Make a sentence strip that says "I did it—on my own!" Color the I's on the sentence strip in a bright color to make them stand out from the other letters:

I dId It — on my own!

3 Show the sentence strip to the class. Have several students read it aloud to familiarize everyone with this positive "I" statement.

4 Pass the strip to individual students and ask each of them to first read it aloud and then tell one thing they are able to do on their own.

Examples:

"I did it—on my own! - - tying my shoelaces."

"I did it—on my own! - - making my bed!"

"I did it—on my own! - - feeding the dog!"

DISCUSS WITH STUDENTS THE IMPORTANCE OF DOING AS MUCH OF THEIR HOMEWORK AS THEY CAN ON THEIR OWN

1 Ask students to tell why they think they should do as much homework as they can on their own.

2 Talk about when it's OK to ask for help. (When they've already tried their best to do the work on their own.)

3 Talk about the kinds of help they sometimes might need from parents or other adults.
- Going over directions.
- Doing the first part together so they understand how to do the rest on their own.
- Doing easier parts first and only asking for help when they get stuck.

4 Ask students to talk about how they feel when they can do school assignments on their own.

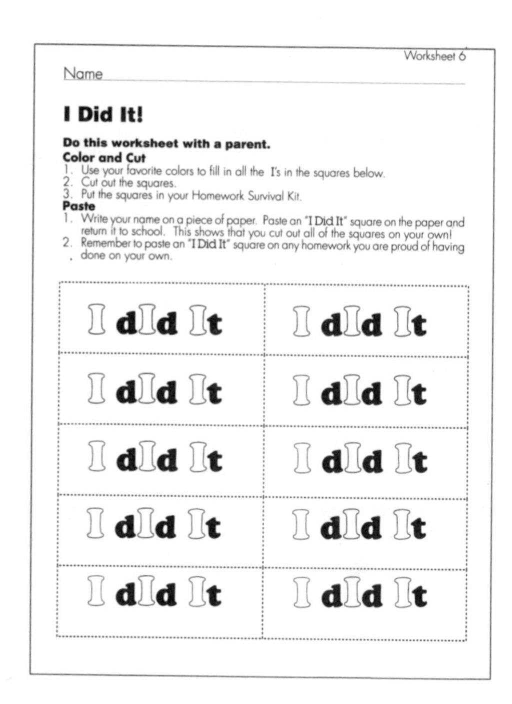
Worksheet 6

Name ______

I Did It!

Do this worksheet with a parent.
Color and Cut
1. Use your favorite colors to fill in all the I's in the squares below.
2. Cut out the squares.
3. Put the squares in your Homework Survival Kit.

Paste
1. Write your name on a piece of paper. Paste an "I Did It" square on the paper and return it to school. This shows that you cut out all of the squares on your own!
2. Remember to paste an "I Did It" square on any homework you are proud of having done on your own.

I did It	I did It
I did It	I did It
I did It	I did It
I did It	I did It
I did It	I did It

EXPLAIN THE HOMEWORK ASSIGNMENT (WORKSHEET 6)

1 Tell students that you are giving them an assignment that will help them take pride in doing homework on their own. Explain that they will be cutting out their own "I Did It " squares . . . just like they read on the sentence strip.

2 Show Worksheet 6: I Did It! Use the sentence strip to model how they will color the "I did it!" statements on the worksheet. Tell students to cut out the squares after they have colored them.

3 Instruct students to put the cut-out squares in an envelope or box to keep them together in their Homework Survival Kit.

4 In order for them to practice using the squares, tell students to write their names on a piece of paper after they have cut out the squares on their own at home. They can then paste one of the "I Did It!" squares on the paper and return it to school.

5 Make sure that students understand that the rest of the squares are to be used whenever they wish to identify a homework assignment that they are proud of having done on their own.

SHOW PARENT TIP SHEET 6

1 Encourage students to compare and talk about what's happening in the cartoons.

2 Read the Parent Tips to them as appropriate.

3 Make sure students take home the Parent Tip Sheet.

FOLLOW UP

1 Create an "I Did It—On My Own!" bulletin board to which you periodically add index card statements of things your students begin to do on their own that they couldn't do on their own earlier in the year. Also add homework assignments that are returned to school with "I Did It!" squares attached.

2 As the year proceeds, give students additional copies of the "I Did It" worksheet for use at home, or have them design "I Did It" squares of their own.

Lesson 7

REWARDING YOURSELF FOR HOMEWORK SUCCESS

RATIONALE

Praise received from others is a powerful motivator. But students must also learn to take pride in their own efforts and to give themselves a personal "pat on the back" when they are pleased with their work. Lesson 7 teaches students the importance of rewarding oneself for a job well done.

OBJECTIVE

Students will choose ways that they can reward themselves for meeting their homework goals.

MATERIALS

Student Worksheet 7a (Appendix page 92), Student Worksheet 7b (Appendix page 93), Parent Tip Sheet 7 (Appendix page 102)

PROCEDURE

INTRODUCE THE CONCEPT OF REWARDING ONESELF FOR A JOB WELL DONE

1. Ask students to tell how they feel when they have done a good job at something. How do they feel when someone praises them or rewards them for doing such a good job?
2. Ask students to talk about times that they have received special praise or a reward for doing a good job at something.
3. Talk about the importance of giving *yourself* a little reward when you've done something you're proud of.
4. Ask students to tell of a time when they've done something special for themselves as a reward for something they have accomplished on their own. What was the reward? How did you feel giving yourself this little "pat on the back"?
5. Why is it a good idea to reward yourself?

DISCUSS WITH STUDENTS THE CONCEPT OF REWARDING THEMSELVES FOR DOING A GOOD JOB ON HOMEWORK

1. Tell students that it's a good idea to reward yourself for doing a good job with homework. Ask them to tell about different times they might reward themselves:

   Examples:

- When I bring homework back on time.
- When I do my homework on my own.
- When I keep my Homework Survival Kit filled.
- When I do my homework without being told to again and again.
- When I do very neat work.

2 Brainstorm ways students can reward themselves. Make sure the students understand that these must be rewards they have the power to give to themselves. Ask each student to suggest one reward that he or she would be able to give himself or herself.

Examples:

- Take a ride on my bike.
- Color a picture.
- Play with my pet.
- Fix myself a snack.
- Read a book.
- Watch a favorite television program.

Worksheet 7a

Name

Ways I Can Reward Myself for Doing a Good Job on Homework

1. Look carefully at all the pictures on this page. Each picture shows something that might be fun to do.
2. Cut out the pictures that show ways you would like to reward yourself for doing a good job on homework. Be sure to choose things that you really could do!
3. In the blank space, draw another way you could reward yourself.

Play with my brother.	Play with my sister.	Call a friend.
Play with a friend.		Play a game.
Play with my pet.	Help fix dinner.	Color a picture.

EXPLAIN THE HOMEWORK ASSIGNMENT (WORKSHEETS 7A AND 7B)

1 Tell students that you are giving them an assignment that will help them think about the different ways they can reward themselves for doing a good job.

2 Pass out Worksheet 7a: Ways I Can Reward Myself for Doing a Good Job on Homework. Tell students that the pictures on this page show some "rewards" that they might give themselves for doing a good job on homework. (Read some of the rewards from the worksheet.)

3 Explain to students that they are to cut out pictures of things they would like to reward themselves with. Point out that there is also a blank square on the page. They may use this space to draw a picture of another reward they might like to give themselves.

4 Show Worksheet 7b: This Is How I Can Reward Myself for Doing a Good Job on Homework. Tell students to paste their "reward squares" in the surprise package.

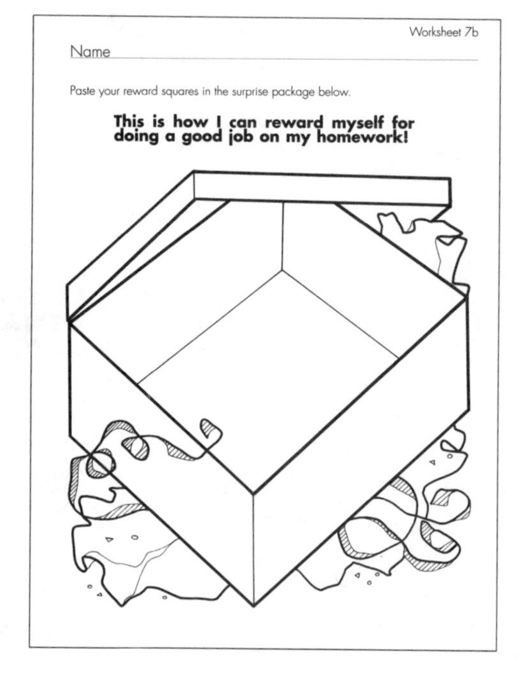

Worksheet 7b

Name

Paste your reward squares in the surprise package below.

This is how I can reward myself for doing a good job on my homework!

SHOW PARENT TIP SHEET 7

Parent Tip Sheet 7

MOTIVATE CHILDREN WITH PRAISE

HOMEWORK WITH TEARS

Children need encouragement and support from the people whose opinions they value the most—their parents. Your consistent praise can encourage your child to feel good about his or her ability *and* motivate your child to do his or her best work.

Each night praise your child about some specific accomplishment. Say something positive about a specific goal your child has set. Example: "I really like how you're doing your homework on your own now."

It is important to **PRAISE** all homework efforts. Let your child know just how proud you are of how hard he or she is working.

HOMEWORK WITHOUT TEARS

Use Super Praise to motivate your child!

First, one parent praises the child: "I really appreciate how hard you're working to do your homework. You finished it all during Daily Homework Time and you did a great job. I want to make sure Dad hears about this when he gets home."

Second, this parent praises the child in front of the other parent: "Patty did a really fine job on her homework today. She started it without complaining, she stayed with it, and she did a super job on it."

Finally, the other parent praises the child: "I really feel proud of you, getting such a good report from Mom. You're really doing fine!"

If you're a single parent, you can use a grandparent, a neighbor, or a family friend as your partner in delivering Super Praise. Any adult whose approval your child will value can fill the role of the second person offering praise.

1. Encourage students to compare and talk about what's happening in the cartoons.
2. Read the Parent Tips to them as appropriate.
3. Make sure students take home the Parent Tip Sheet.

FOLLOW UP

1. Return completed worksheets to students. Tell them to keep the sheet in their Homework Survival Kit as a reminder of ways to reward themselves when they've done a terrific job on homework!
2. As the year goes on, encourage students to share ways they've rewarded themselves for things they are proud of having done.

Chapter 4

4 STEPS TO GIVING EFFECTIVE HOMEWORK ASSIGNMENTS

Chapter 3 of this book provides lessons to teach your students how to do homework responsibly. But that's only part of the picture. The ultimate quality of your homework program—and its benefit to your students—depends upon the *effectiveness* of the homework assignments you give.

Homework is **not** effective when it is hastily assigned as students are walking out the door at the end of the day.

Homework is **not** effective when it has no learning objective.

Homework is **not** effective when it bears no connection to classroom lessons.

Homework is **not** effective when students do not have the necessary skills to complete it independently.

Keep in mind that each time you give a homework assignment you are asking three groups of people—yourself, your students, and their parents— to invest their time and energy. It is, therefore, extremely important that your homework assignments warrant this investment—and that time is being used to its maximum advantage.

What determines an effective homework assignment?

To be utilized as an effective educational tool, homework must be recognized as a *process*. The homework process begins when you first plan your classroom lesson. This is the time when you should focus on the objective of the homework assignment you intend to give. The process continues as you decide the *type* of assignment to give, as you create or choose that assignment, and as you introduce it to the class. The homework process doesn't end until the assignment has been collected, commented upon or graded and returned to the student.

Each step of this process is a vital component of an effective homework assignment.

To help guide you through the homework process, *Homework Without Tears for Teachers* provides the following 4 Steps to Giving Effective Homework Assignments:

Step 1: Determine the learning objective of the homework assignment you are going to give.

Step 2: Make sure the homework assignment you choose fits the homework learning objective.

Step 3: Introduce the assignment to students clearly and effectively.

Step 4: Follow a pre-determined plan for collecting and correcting homework efficiently and in a time-saving manner.

STEP 1: Determine the learning objective of your homework assignment.

Before you give any homework assignment, you must first know exactly *why* you are giving it. To ensure that homework is more than busywork, you must clearly determine your learning objectives. You must ask yourself, "Why am I giving this assignment?"

Is your objective to have students **review and practice** specific skills or material learned in class?

Is your objective to **prepare** your students for an upcoming class topic?

Is your objective to have students **apply skills** or concepts learned in class to new situations?

When you take time to determine the objective of your assignment, you will:

1. Give yourself the opportunity to make sure that the learning objective is really worth pursuing. Are students going to learn from this task, or will they be filling their time and heads with unimportant facts or details?
2. Make sure that the learning objective is appropriate for all students.
3. Choose or design the type of assignment that would best fulfill the learning objective.

Note: Get into the habit of giving as much thought to your homework assignments as you do to your classroom lessons. The best time to plan your homework is when you are planning the lesson. Look at the homework assignment as an extension and enhancement of a specific lesson. Record your homework assignments in your planbook right alongside the day's lesson. Take time to evaluate the flow of homework within one subject area. Is it leading somewhere, or is it simply a disorganized potpourri of tasks?

STEP 2: Make sure the homework assignment you choose fits the homework learning objective.

Your learning objective will determine the type of assignment you give. Homework assignments in grades 1-3 generally fall into three categories:

Practice Homework

Preparation Homework

Extension Homework

Practice Homework
Objective: To review and practice specific skills or materials covered in class.

Practice assignments are the most commonly given homework, particularly in lower grades. Because practice assignments can be readily given through supplemental worksheets as well as textbooks, they can also be the most easily misused and *overused* type of homework. Don't fall into the trap of handing out practice worksheets or other drill work just to give out homework.

Keep in mind that your goal in giving a practice assignment must be to practice a *particular* skill that *has been covered in class*. Don't assign practice homework that is a conglomeration of lots of skills. For homework to be effective, the students must clearly be able to see what skill they are practicing.

Examples of practice homework assignments:

"Circle the pictures that have the long a sound."

"Write the plurals of the words on this page."

"Do problems 1 - 12 on page 60."

"Use each of this week's spelling words in a sentence."

When should you assign practice homework?

Ask yourself: Is my objective to have students review and reinforce specific skills or material they have learned in class? Do the students *need* to practice this skill? Have they already mastered this skill?

Guidelines for Assigning More Effective Practice Homework Assignments

- Don't give practice assignments if students do not need to practice that skill.
- Make sure that the practice assignment covers material covered in class.
- Assign practice homework only after you have determined that the student can do the work with reasonable success. Don't expect parents to "teach" skills to their children.
- Make sure a practice assignment focuses on a particular skill.
- Don't overdo drill assignments. Keep in mind that students who already grasp a concept don't need the practice, and would be better served and challenged by other types of homework. (Example: Why ask a student who already knows how to spell a word to write it ten times?) Likewise, students who don't understand a concept will just be reinforcing errors.
- Because it's sometimes difficult to be certain just who did a practice assignment (Mom, Dad, sister, brother, or the student), it's a good idea to occasionally follow such assignments with a quiz to determine if learning is taking place.
- Avoid the temptation to hand out "last-minute" practice worksheets just because you haven't planned anything else. Any homework is **not** better than no homework at all.

Additional Ideas for Improving the Effectiveness of Practice Homework

Assigning practice homework that matches your students' varied abilities *and* also raises their level of thinking need not require greater amounts of teacher preparation time. You can still give textbook assignments and utilize supplemental and workbook worksheets. However, *how* you use these materials is one of the keys to assigning more effective homework.

Here are some ways to use textbooks and workbooks creatively and at the appropriate level:

- Instead of assigning all students the same 20-problem page, have each student select 3 or 5 problems on the page that show what they are able to do.
- Set a time limit that each student is expected to spend on a homework assignment and accept the number of problems the student does in that time. Have a parent signature verify the time.
- Instead of assigning 20 problems on a page, have students do the top 3, middle 3, and bottom 3.
- Have students complete a few math problems in their text and then write more of their own on the same concept.
- Instead of *defining* spelling words, have students use the words in sentences, a poem or creative story.
- Have students select 5 words (for example) from a story they have read in their reading book. Give them specifics for choosing these words: words that describe how people feel; words that describe how things look; words that describe how things move, etc. If appropriate, have students write the words in alphabetical order.
- After reading a story in the reader, ask students to draw a picture of a different ending to the story.
- Have students draw a picture that represents a specific math problem.

Preparation Homework
Objective: To prepare students for an upcoming class topic.

Preparation homework is given when you want students to prepare on their own for an upcoming lesson. Properly assigned, preparation homework can serve to stimulate interest in the upcoming topic.

Examples of preparation homework:

"Collect three different leaves from trees or plants around your home. Bring these leaves to class."

"Find a picture in a magazine that shows one way people travel from place to place. Cut out the picture and bring it to class."

"Ask your parent to help you write down one rule for going safely to and from school. Bring your rule to class."

Note: Each of the preparation homework examples above asks the student to obtain specific information as an objective. Since the homework is covering new material, it is important that the student knows why he or she is doing this assignment.

When should you assign preparation homework?

Ask yourself: Is my goal to prepare students for an upcoming class topic? Will I follow up this assignment with related material in class?

Guidelines for Assigning More Effective Preparation Homework Assignments

- Make sure that your assignment is specific. Students must understand before they begin *why* they are doing this assignment.
- *Always* follow up a preparation homework assignment with a related lesson in class.
- Use a variety of sources for preparation homework assignments: magazine pictures, TV, parents.

Extension Homework
Objective: To apply concepts or skills learned in class to new situations.

The most meaningful and motivating learning occurs when students are asked to *apply* what they have learned in school to other situations. Homework, because it's done away from the classroom, provides the perfect opportunity for students to practice this transfer of learning. (A recognized goal of education is for students to be able to transfer learning from one context to another.) An extension homework assignment is one of the best uses you can make of homework.

Examples of extension homework:

"Interview your parent. Ask him or her to talk about . . . ."

"Pretend that the main character in (the story we read today) came home with you for a day. What would you do? What would you talk about? What would the visit be like? Draw a picture that shows you and your new friend. Write a sentence to go with the picture."

"Plan a dinner menu for your family. Make sure that you choose foods from the four basic food groups." (For younger children, have them cut out magazine pictures to show their menu.)

When should you assign extension homework?

Ask yourself: Is my goal to have students apply what they have learned in class to new situations?

Guidelines for Assigning More Effective Extension Homework Assignments

- Keep in mind that any subject matter is appropriate for extension homework.
- Brainstorm with students to come up with ways that they can apply what they've learned in school to other situations.
- Try to give extension homework as often as possible.
- See the Creative Homework Models (Chapter 7) for ideas for extension assignments. Start off with these lessons and you'll soon be coming up with lots more of your own!

Additional points to keep in mind when designing and choosing homework assignments:

The homework assignment must not require the student to do something he or she does not know how to do.

Before a homework assignment is given, you must determine that each student has the skills (and, perhaps, resources) necessary to do the work. Keep in mind that most homework assignments are expected to be done independently. It makes no sense to give a student an independent assignment that he or she lacks the skills to complete.

The assignment is not too much or too long.

Don't fall into the "more is better" trap. (This is particularly applicable to practice assignments.) Keep your objective for the assignment in mind. If, for example, 5 problems will let you know whether or not a student understands a specific math concept, why ask for 20? Remember: If a student clearly grasps a concept he or she doesn't need the practice. If the student does *not* understand the concept, he or she will just be reinforcing errors.

The written directions are clear and concise.

Few things are as frustrating to students (and their parents) as incomprehensible directions. If directions to a second grader, for example, are meant to be read by that second grader, then make sure they are not written at a sixth-grade level. Take time to re-read your directions.

Homework time will be spent on *learning.*

Don't waste student time on non-learning tasks. For example, don't ask students to copy questions, *then* write the answers. They are not learning anything while copying. Instead, have them answer the questions in a complete sentence that explains what is being asked. (Likewise writing spelling words ten times each.)

Homework should never be used as a disciplinary consequence.

Giving homework as a punishment is never appropriate. Remember that your homework goal is for learning to take place, and for the student to be a willing, capable participant in that learning. When you assign homework as a disciplinary consequence you confuse this goal with a negative factor, and only increase the likelihood that students will look upon homework with a less than enthusiastic response.

Keep in mind that the most effective homework program is one that consists of a variety of types of homework assignments. Just as your students at times need to review and practice skills learned in class, they also need to have the opportunity to extend those same skills and apply them to other situations. When planning homework assignments, continue to ask yourself: "Will my students really learn appropriately from this assignment?" After all, if the student doesn't learn anything, there's no reason to give it.

STEP 3: Introduce the homework assignment clearly.

How you present your homework assignments to your students can be as important to the effectiveness of the assignment as the type of homework you assign. Research has shown that the way homework is presented affects the frequency with which students complete the homework and the motivation of students to do a good job on their homework assignments.

You can improve the effectiveness of your homework assignments—and increase your students' homework achievement— by following the simple guidelines below:

Always discuss the purpose of each assignment by saying, "Doing this homework will help you to (for example) correctly use commas. . . ." (Preparing for this step will also help *you* make certain there is a clear objective for the assignment.)

Give clear, concise directions both orally and, if appropriate, in written form. Don't write an assignment on the board without discussion or explanation. At the same time, don't expect students to remember directions that are only given orally. You can explain the assignment orally, but you should also write the directions on the board or on the top part of the homework worksheet, if applicable.

Write homework assignments in the same place each day. For older students, designate a portion of the board as the "homework corner" and keep the assignments up all week so students who are absent can readily determine their make-up work.

Make sure you allow enough time for students to ask questions about the assignment. Don't wait until the last minute to give the homework assignment. Don't assume that students understand what is required of them just because they haven't asked many questions. To check on understanding, ask students to repeat the directions in their own words.

When appropriate, show samples of a successfully completed assignment to model what is expected or draw diagrams or pictures of what the final product should look like.

When appropriate, allow the students to start the homework assignment in class. If there is any confusion, the class can do a small part of the assignment together. You can help answer questions as they arise or ask students who understand the directions to model how they are doing the assignment.

Review the homework policy with your class on a frequent basis. Remind the students how the policy will be enforced when assignments are incomplete or late. Be consistent with consequences and make-up procedures, especially at the start of the school year when patterns are being set and with students who are testing the limits of your homework policy.

Continue to emphasize to students the importance of homework. Reinforce this importance by collecting and correcting all or most of the homework assignments.

Try other "homework helper" ideas to further ensure student success with homework.

Institute a study hour after school.

This is particularly helpful for students who do not have a quiet place in which to study at home.

Assign a homework "study buddy" to each student.

Tell students to check with their study buddy when they are unsure of an assignment, or need to work through a problem with someone else. Make sure that study buddies exchange phone numbers!

Create a Homework Hotline for your class or school.

A Homework Hotline, staffed by teacher or community volunteers, gives each student the opportunity of having a supportive, helpful hand when they need it. This is especially beneficial for students who are on their own after school and are having specific problems with a homework assignment.

STEP 4: Use time-saving tips for collecting and correcting homework.

Collecting Homework

Finding efficient ways to collect students' homework assignments on a daily or weekly basis can save time and effort when it comes time to correct the homework. The suggestions that follow can be adapted to your own personal classroom style.

Have each student make a construction paper or manila file folder with his or her name on it. Each student should keep all completed homework in the folder at all times for daily, weekly or random checks. These personal homework folders can be stored in students' desks, or in a designated place in the classroom.

Make a different color-coded construction paper folder for each day of the week or each subject area. Make the students responsible for getting homework into the correct folders.

Make a dated folder for each day's (or each week's) homework assignments. Staple a copy of your class list inside each folder so you—or the students—can quickly check off or initial who's completed the homework on time. In this way, you can immediately reinforce those students who have met homework deadlines while following through on consequences for those with late or missed assignments, per your homework policy.

Clear off a countertop or book shelf and use masking tape labels to indicate which homework assignments go where. You can increase the likelihood of homework papers getting in the right place by using boxes (empty manila folder boxes are exactly the right size) to hold the assignments.

Assign a row or table monitor each week to collect homework.

Have homework handed in or collected the same time each day. Examples: When the late bell rings all homework should be on the desk ready to be collected; Before going to reading group, place homework in the appropriate folder.

Correcting Homework

Research indicates that it is vitally important that you collect all homework and either grade it or comment on it. Not every assignment must be graded, but the students must know that homework will be checked and commented upon in some way. Finding efficient ways to correct students' homework assignments can help you give students needed feedback on a consistent basis and, at the same time, can give you relief from "homework burnout."

Keep in mind that you can always shorten your correction time by balancing the types of assignments you give:

- Assignments that require students to "tell some information" in class vs. those that require work shown on paper.
- Assignments that students can correct themselves vs. those that you or an aide correct.
- Assignments that require grades vs. those that only need comments.
- Assignments that require students to bring something to class to share vs. those that require written descriptions.

The #1 Homework Correcting Rule

Whenever possible, comment in a positive way on how each student did on an assignment. Positive comments produce the best results! By commenting on the homework, you are letting students know that you place enough importance on their work to give it your time

Summary

It is clear that the homework process requires a commitment from all involved. Assigning effective homework is your part of that commitment. When you take the time to ensure that the assignments you give are as effective as possible, you are ensuring in your classroom that homework means learning is taking place.

Chapter 5

HOW TO MOTIVATE STUDENTS TO DO THEIR HOMEWORK

Once you have taught students how to do homework and begin sending home assignments, you must provide motivation for students to complete homework on a regular basis.

For students who have had good school experiences and receive recognition at home, getting good grades may be motivation enough for them to do their homework. But the rest of your students may need something more to motivate them to complete homework. The most powerful motivational tool available to you is positive reinforcement.

Recognizing and rewarding appropriate behavior encourages students to continue that behavior. Students are more likely to continue to do homework when you give them praise for homework completed to your expectations. A simple "Thank you for turning your homework in on time" can go a long way toward encouraging students to continue their good work.

Positive reinforcement can also change behavior. When you have students who occasionally do not do their homework, give them extra attention or special privileges on days when they do complete their assignments. With students who only now and then miss homework assignments, it is important to concentrate on positives when they choose to do their work. Many times these students are just looking for attention. Therefore, make sure they receive more attention when they do their assignments than when they don't do them.

By praising students for doing a good job on homework, you make them feel better about their own abilities. And as you increase students' confidence and raise their self-image, you encourage them to do their assignments by themselves and to the best of their abilities.

Keep in mind that positive reinforcement must be:

- Something the students like.
- Something you are comfortable using.
- Something used on a consistent basis.

Don't underestimate the power of positive reinforcement. Because of their home environment or previous experiences in school, many students lack and crave positive recognition. Your positive comments, notes and other incentives could be deciding factors in a student's self-confidence and success in school.

In the early grades you are setting the stage for the years to follow when there is a greater amount of homework and more is expected of the student. It is, therefore, especially important for your students to succeed at homework. And it is up to you to motivate them to succeed.

Positive Reinforcement You Can Give to Individual Students

Verbal praise

An effective form of reinforcement for doing homework is praise. Praise is appreciated by all children. It is particularly important for those students who are hard to motivate. Many children who do not do homework feel insecure in their ability to succeed in anything relating to school. Keep in mind the enormous impact your praise can have on their self-esteem. With continual positive support, you can motivate students to develop a positive self-image and to approach homework with a confident, I-can-do-it attitude.

Use praise often and remember:

- Praise should be specific. For example, "John, your description of the storm in your story was terrific. I could almost feel the wind as I read it," rather than, "Good job, John."
- To be most effective, praise must be used consistently. Give positive comments on content of homework rather than just appearances.

Positive comments on completed homework

For many students, your constant praise is enough to stimulate and sustain enthusiasm about homework. But other children are more difficult to motivate with words alone. With these children, positive notes on their assignments can be very effective.

When you check homework:

- Add stickers, happy faces or other kinds of reinforcers for the students.
- Add positive, specific comments not just at the top of the homework paper, but throughout the assignment.

Oftentimes, a note of praise from you can be a much more powerful motivator than a good grade. Your notes not only tell students that you care about their *work* ("Karen, you put a lot of effort into this job. You really understood the lesson!"), but they also let students know that you care about *them* ("Bob, this is neatly done. I am proud of you!"). Remember, especially with hard-to-motivate students, building their self-esteem is key to helping them succeed.

Positive notes to parents

Students of all grade levels appreciate notes sent to their parents recognizing that they have done a good job on homework. (See Appendix page 103 for Positive Notes for Parents.) Also, if parents are fulfilling their role in supporting homework, they too will appreciate knowing that their efforts are paying off. It is important that you make positive contact with parents on a regular basis.

When using positive notes to parents:

- Set a goal to send home a certain number of notes per week.
- Be specific with your praise, "Jenny has been doing an excellent job following homework directions this week. You should be very proud of her."

Building a positive relationship with parents will also make it easier for you when you have to contact them about a problem. If you regularly send home positive notes, you communicate to the parents that you care about their children's success.

Homework cards

This method of reinforcement allows individual students to earn points toward a reward each time a homework assignment is completed.

- Place a card on each student's desk. The card is divided into ten or twenty boxes.
- Each day that homework is completed, place a check or a sticker in one of the boxes.
- When the entire card is filled, the student earns a reward such as extra free time, an award certificate or a tasty treat.

Reinforcement Ideas You Can Use for the Entire Class

Here are two great ideas on how to set up positive reinforcement systems for your entire classroom. (Remember, the reward systems must be built around something the students like.) Below are examples of the types of systems teachers have found both fun and effective.

Bulletin boards to display student homework

By using a bulletin board featuring homework, you are giving the entire class a constant reminder of the importance you place on homework. Also, when you use the bulletin board to display homework that is done well, you are providing more positive reinforcement. All students enjoy seeing their good work posted for everyone to see. When using a homework bulletin board:

- Introduce how you are going to use the bulletin board when you present your homework policy to your students. (To display the best papers by row, etc.)
- Change the papers on the board weekly to allow as many students as possible to have their work displayed.

Homework chart

You can also set up a positive reinforcement system for the entire class by posting a homework chart on your bulletin board. The chart lists all of the students and provides a place to check every time a homework assignment is turned in on time. When the entire class turns in assignments on a given day, the class earns a point. When a certain number of points (5-10) are earned, the entire class gets a special privilege. This system is also effective because of the peer pressure it creates for all students to turn in homework on time. The guidelines for using a homework chart are:

- Every time all students turn in a completed homework assignment, one point is earned by the class.
- When a predetermined number of points is reached, the class earns a reward such as extra free time, a popcorn party or an extended recess.
- Make sure that rewards can be earned in a relatively short period of time.

Using a homework chart also gives you an excellent means of documenting homework completed and not completed. Since the chart covers several weeks, it also allows you to spot patterns that show if students continually have trouble completing homework on a certain day.

Summary

Positive reinforcement is one of the most effective tools at your disposal to ensure your students' success in school. Because it is so important, you should not leave your use of positives to chance. In addition to putting positive notes on students' homework, set a goal for yourself to send home at least two positive notes to parents each day.

These notes will not only motivate students to do homework, they will also build a positive relationship between you and the parents. One of the keys to effective homework is recognizing and encouraging the efforts of everyone involved in the homework process.

Chapter 6

WHAT TO DO IF STUDENTS DO NOT COMPLETE HOMEWORK

For young students, the consistent use of positive reinforcement for individual students and the entire class is the most powerful motivator you have to help them develop good homework habits. However, if you consistently use the motivational ideas in the previous chapter and still have students who do not complete their homework, you cannot ignore the problem. You must determine how you can help the student succeed. Are there circumstances beyond the child's control that prevent him or her from completing the homework?

Some students may be embarrassed to tell you that they couldn't do their homework because no one is at home or because life at home is so unsettled that it is difficult to complete anything in that environment. If you suspect a problem, you may want to talk with the parents to find out what the problem is.

With young students it is especially important to involve the parents the minute you see a pattern of poor homework habits developing that indicates homework is not being completed or is being done in a haphazard manner. The parents can be your best allies and together you can work on helping the student to achieve success.

This chapter presents two approaches you can use to help all students complete their homework.

- In Part One, you are given phone scripts to use when contacting parents and a checklist to help parents motivate their children to complete homework.
- In Part Two, you are given techniques that you can use at school should you not be able to get support at home or if that support is not working.

Note: Any technique you plan to use with students who do not complete homework must be clearly explained in your homework policy.

Before taking any action for homework not completed, the following questions need to be answered:

- Have you thoroughly explained homework assignments? Are the assignments appropriate to the student's grade level and do they only cover material already explained in class? (Review the guidelines in Chapter 4 on how to assign effective homework.)
- Are you sure that the student does not have a learning disability that is preventing him or her from completing homework?
- Are you sure that nothing has changed in the home environment to prevent the student from doing homework? (Has the student demonstrated the ability in class to do the work but is unable to do it at home?)
- Do you collect and check homework on a regular basis?
- Do you provide positive reinforcement on a regular basis?

If you have answered "yes" to all of the above questions, and still have students who are not doing their homework, it is time for you to contact the parents.

PART ONE: WHAT PARENTS CAN DO AT HOME TO SOLVE HOMEWORK PROBLEMS

Many parents are at a loss for what to do at home to ensure that their children complete their homework assignments. It is important, therefore, that you supply the parents with the knowledge and skills they need to deal with their children. Remember, all parents want their children to succeed. The more you help parents, the more they will be able to help their children.

Above all, you must clearly tell parents that the homework habits developed in early grades stay with students for a long time. Both you and the parents must do whatever is needed to see that those habits are responsible ones. If completing homework becomes a recurring problem, both you and the parents will have to take action.

First of all, parents must make homework a number-one, non-negotiable priority. Parents can negotiate bedtime and play time but homework time is non-negotiable. If students have a problem with homework that positive reinforcement does not solve, then stronger action is called for. Not only do you need to impose consequences at school, parents also need to take away privileges at home. When students see that you and the parents are working together, they will be more motivated to do their homework assignments.

Steps to Positive Parent Support

There are specific steps you can take that will help you receive the support of parents:

Communicate your expectations to parents.

To be certain that parents know your expectations both for them and for their children, you must establish a homework policy and send that policy home to parents. (See Chapter 2.)

Establish positive communication with parents.

Parents often develop a negative attitude toward teachers and school because they are contacted only when their child has misbehaved or is doing poorly. You can change this attitude by providing positive feedback and establishing positive communication. This can be accomplished by sending positive notes home consistently and by making positive phone calls.

Document homework problems.

In order to present an accurate professional picture of a student's work, you must keep accurate records of specific homework problems and how often they occur. You are more likely to get parental support if you can specifically describe the problem rather than deal in generalities.

Contact parents at the first sign of a problem.

Probably the most common mistake in working with parents is that teachers do not contact them about a problem until the problem is out of hand. Contact parents at the first sign of a problem. As soon as you realize a student is having problems with homework that necessitates involving the parents, call them.

Before contacting parents, plan what you will say.

Planning what you will say before contacting parents is essential to make sure that you are effectively communicating the situation.

Make sure that parents understand that your number-one reason for calling is your concern for their child. When you show this concern, you maximize your opportunity to get parental support.

Follow these specific guidelines when contacting parents:

- **Describe the behavior that necessitated your call.**

  Describe in specific, observable terms what the child did or did not do. Phrases like "His homework is not acceptable" or "She is having a problem with homework" are not observable. Use comments like:

  "I am calling because I'm very concerned about Walter. He did not turn in three homework assignments this week."

  "I am calling because Nancy consistently turns in homework assignments that are not complete."

- **Describe what you have done to help the child.**

  Clearly spell out that you have taken action on your own before contacting the parent.

  "As stated in my homework policy, I have praised your child when he does complete homework and had him stay in at recess to complete unfinished work."

  "From your child's performance in class, I know she is capable of completing these assignments. I have discussed the problem with her and had her complete her assignments during lunch."

- **Describe what you want the parent to do.**

  Always preface what you want the parent to do with the statement, "It is in your child's best interest that we work together to help him (her). For example:

  "It is in your child's best interest that she knows that we are working together to help her complete all homework assignments. As she is having a recurring problem completing homework, I want you to support my efforts by taking away privileges like TV or playing until her homework is done. The homework habits your daughter develops at this early age will stay with her for a long time. It is important then that we help her develop responsible habits."

- **Indicate your confidence in your ability to solve the problem if the parent works with you. Indicate that the parent's support is critical.**

  "I am sure that if we work together we will be able to motivate your child to do his homework on his own."

  "I am sure that if we work together we will most definitely help your daughter complete all of her homework assignments."

- **Indicate that there will be follow-up contact from you.**

  Let the parent know that you will not let the issue drop, and that you will be in touch within one week to inform the parent if the situation has or has not improved.

  "I'll be back in touch with you in a week, either by phone or with a note, to let you know how things are going."

  "I want to make sure we deal with this problem before it becomes more serious. I will let you know in a week how your daughter is doing."

If necessary, send home the "How to Handle Homework Problems" parent checklist.

To help parents deal with their children more effectively, *Homework Without Tears for Teachers* provides you with a checklist to give to parents to help them solve the most common homework problems. This checklist gives parents step-by-step solutions to most of the homework problems they may face. The "How to Handle Homework Problems" checklist is found in the Appendix, pages 107-110, and tells parents what to do if:

Children will not do their best work.
Children refuse to do homework.
Children fail to bring assignments home.
Children take all night to finish homework.
Children will not do homework on their own.
Children will not do homework if parents are not home.

How to Use the Parent Checklist

The "How to Handle Homework Problems" parent checklist is a step-by-step guide that can be "personalized" to meet the needs of individual students. It can be used most effectively in a conference situation. Go through the steps outlined with the parent, following this sequence:

1 Review the parent's past actions regarding homework. Has the parent made sure that the home environment is conducive to doing homework effectively?

2 Work with the parent to pinpoint the problem the child is having. Check the response square in part 2 that describes that specific problem.

3 Now encourage the parent to tell his or her child exactly what is expected. Check the response square in part 3 that corresponds to the problem.

4 Emphasize to the parent that praise is a powerful motivator. Check the response square in part 4 that corresponds to the child's problem.

5 Talk to the parent about providing additional incentives that will help get the child into the habit of doing homework appropriately. Three incentive ideas are presented on the sheet: the Homework Contract, the "Beat the Clock" game, and the "Chunking" strategy. Check the one(s) that you feel will best help the child.

6 Explain that if homework expectations are still not met, then the parent must "back up words with action" by letting the child know that his or her behavior will result in a loss of privileges. Discuss with the parent various options, such as no TV or no playing after school until homework is completed.

7 Emphasize your willingness to continue to work with the parent to solve homework problems. Explain that, if need be, there are measures you can take at school that can help support the parent.

Add any additional comments to the final page of the checklist that you feel might be helpful to the parent. Give the checklist to the parent, encouraging him or her to keep it as a handy reference for solving homework problems now, and those that might come up in the future. Set a time (in a week or two) to follow up with the parent to determine whether the strategy has been effective or if further action is necessary.

PART TWO: WHAT YOU CAN DO AT SCHOOL WHEN STUDENTS DO NOT COMPLETE HOMEWORK

If you have involved the parents and the student is still having a problem, then you need to support the parents' efforts by taking action at school. There are various techniques that are typically used by teachers with students who do not complete their homework assignments. Choose the techniques that you feel are appropriate for you and your students.

No matter what techniques you choose, you must have a means of keeping track of homework completed and not completed. Most teachers use their class record books to keep track of homework. It is important that you have these records available when contacting parents. You should also keep a record of notes sent home to parents and of any disciplinary action (missed recess, etc.) taken with the student.

When determining the techniques you will use when students do not complete homework, keep in mind the techniques must:

- Be described in your homework policy.
- Be something you are comfortable using.
- Be such that they apply equally to all students.

Parent-Teacher notes

To solve recurring homework problems, you must have a means of keeping parents involved on an ongoing basis. Sending notes home to parents that require a response is an effective way to motivate both students and parents. (See Appendix page 104.)

If you use this technique, be sure to include positive comments as often as possible. Parents need feedback to know that their efforts are being successful. They also need to be reminded to praise their children when homework is completed.

If you are using the notes to communicate a problem, remember to always include exactly what it is you want the parents to do. For instance, if a student is continually forgetting to bring homework back to school, you might ask the parent to make sure that the student is using the Homework Drop Spot. (See Lesson 2, page 17.)

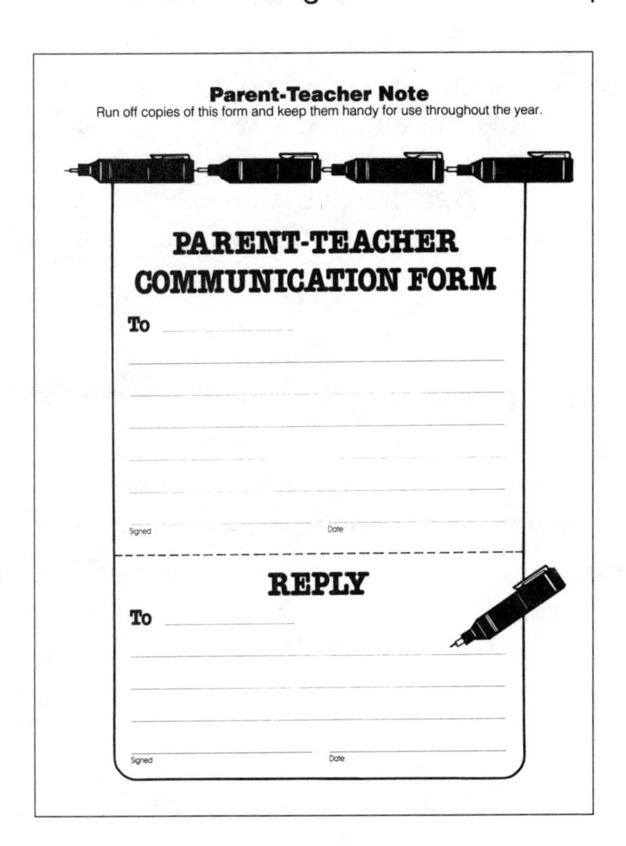

Parent-Teacher Note

Run off copies of this form and keep them handy for use throughout the year.

PARENT-TEACHER COMMUNICATION FORM

To

Signed Date

REPLY

To

Signed Date

Homework calendar

Providing parents with a homework calendar can increase the effectiveness of their involvement with homework. A weekly or monthly calendar lists all homework assignments for the class or for a particular child. The parents can use the calendar to make sure that family activities do not conflict with homework nights and to give them a means of checking to make sure that all assignments are completed. If you are already using a calendar and problems are continuing, ask parents to review and sign completed homework assignments each night.

Simply involving parents in either of these ways will solve many problems because it lets students know that you and the parents are working together to make sure all homework is completed.

Missed recess

A common technique is to have students make up missed homework during recess or lunch recess. If you use loss of free time to make up homework, make sure that:

- Students finish their incomplete work by themselves.
- Talking is not allowed.
- No assistance is given from a teacher or supervisor. This is not helping time.

Note: If a student is always spending lunch or recess time doing homework, this may indicate that there is a problem at home that is preventing him or her from working there. If you suspect this, it is time to contact the parents. Also, younger students often enjoy spending time with the teacher and will miss homework just to get extra time with you. Make sure that you provide one-to-one contact in a way other than during disciplinary time.

Summary

When dealing with students who are having problems getting homework done, remember that the most powerful technique you can use is positive reinforcement. Give them extra praise and recognition those times when they do complete homework.

If extra positives don't solve the problem, use techniques such as the ones suggested in this chapter to let students know that missing homework will not be tolerated. And whatever technique you choose to use, you must use it consistently every time a homework assignment is missed.

Chapter 7
CREATIVE HOMEWORK MODELS

Most textbook and workbook assignments are designed at the practice and review level. However, the most meaningful and motivating learning occurs when students are asked to extend (apply) what they have learned in school to other situations in their lives. Homework, because it's done at home, provides the perfect opportunity for students to extend their learning.

The *Homework Without Tears for Teachers* Creative Homework Models supply a variety of formats for extension homework assignments in which *you* supply the content topic and the *students* apply what they have learned about that topic. The same Homework Model formats can be used over and over again for different subjects with different content specifics.

See the examples below and on the next page:

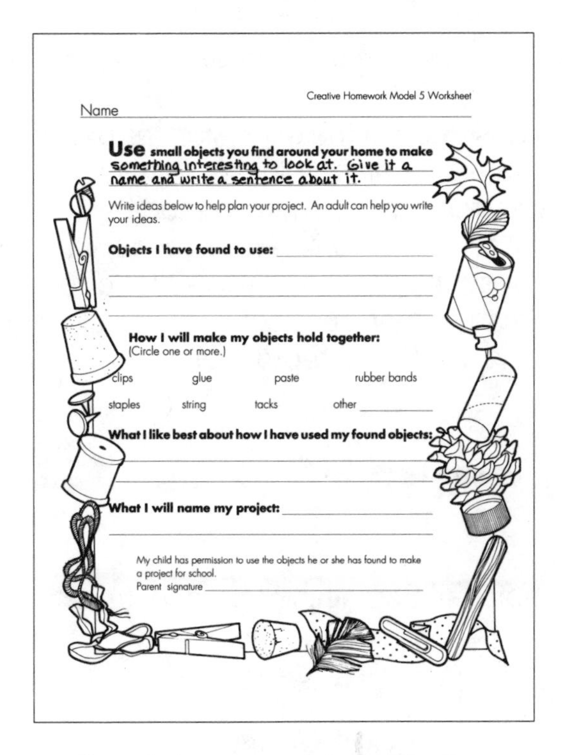

Creative Homework Model 5 Worksheet

Name

Use small objects you find around your home to make something interesting to look at. Give it a name and write a sentence about it.

Write ideas below to help plan your project. An adult can help you write your ideas.

Objects I have found to use:

How I will make my objects hold together:
(Circle one or more.)

clips glue paste rubber bands
staples string tacks other

What I like best about how I have used my found objects:

What I will name my project:

My child has permission to use the objects he or she has found to make a project for school.
Parent signature

Sample Language Arts Application

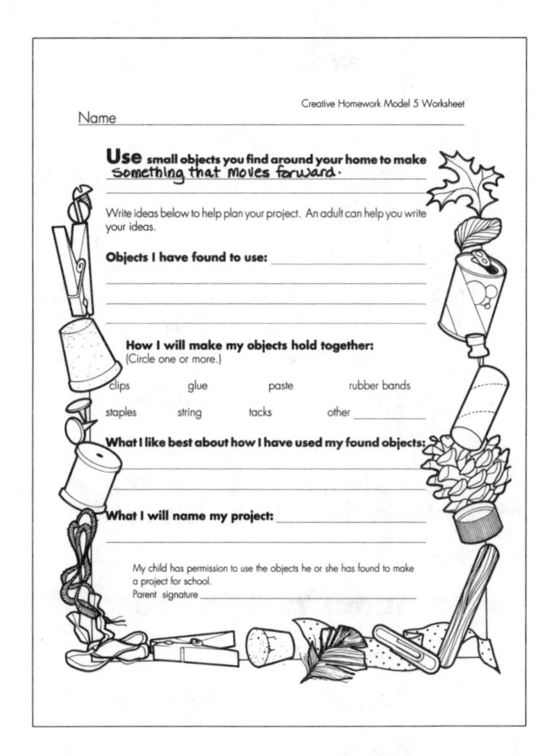

Creative Homework Model 5 Worksheet

Name

Use small objects you find around your home to make something that moves forward.

Write ideas below to help plan your project. An adult can help you write your ideas.

Objects I have found to use:

How I will make my objects hold together:
(Circle one or more.)

clips glue paste rubber bands
staples string tacks other

What I like best about how I have used my found objects:

What I will name my project:

My child has permission to use the objects he or she has found to make a project for school.
Parent signature

Sample Science Application

Creative Homework Model 4 Worksheet

Name

Tell **someone at home 3 things you learned today about** how to use a ruler to measure things.

Try to use full sentences. Write down what you said in the 3 spaces below. Have a parent sign this sheet.

My child told me 3 things that were learned in school today.
Parent signature

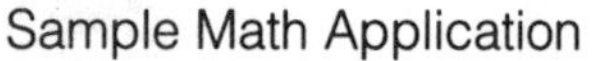

Sample Math Application

Creative Homework Model 4 Worksheet

Name

Tell **someone at home 3 things you learned today about** a firefighter's job.

Try to use full sentences. Write down what you said in the 3 spaces below. Have a parent sign this sheet.

My child told me 3 things that were learned in school today.
Parent signature

Sample Social Studies Application

Each of the Creative Homework Models is designed at the extension (application) level to encourage students to really make learning relevant by seeing its application outside the classroom. As you examine the Homework Models, you will see that application of learning occurs when students *sort, make a model, cut and paste,* etc. The teacher's pages that follow describe each Homework Model format, show sample variations of use, and list many other suggestions for using the worksheets in different subject areas. The blackline reproducible pages are located in the Appendix, pages 113-117.

The Following Creative Homework Models Are Included In This Chapter:

Model 1: Cutting and Pasting Examples of Something Learned
Model 2: Sequencing
Model 3: Categorizing and Sorting
Model 4: Telling Something Learned in Your Own Words
Model 5: Using Found Objects to Make a Model of Something Learned

Creative Homework Model 1

CUTTING AND PASTING EXAMPLES OF SOMETHING LEARNED

This homework sheet is designed to be used for a variety of cutting and pasting activities in which young students are asked to find pictures from home as examples of something they learned in school.

BEFORE YOU BEGIN

Make one copy of the Creative Homework Model 1 worksheet (Appendix page 113). Write in the specific directions you want your students to follow. (See the examples below.) Use this "master" to make a copy of the assignment for each student in your class.

EXPLAIN THE ASSIGNMENT TO STUDENTS

Tell students that they are to use old magazines or newspapers to find pictures of things that (give your assignment). Explain that they are to cut these pictures out and paste them on the worksheet. (Hold up worksheet and show where pictures are to be pasted.) **Note:** If any of your students do not have access to magazines at home, let them take magazines from a class collection home to do this assignment. Be sure to have them bring the magazines back for future use.

APPLICATION

This cutting and pasting activity can be effectively used in different subject areas. You can probably think of many ways to use this homework sheet that will fit your specific curriculum needs and homework learning objectives. Here are some suggestions:

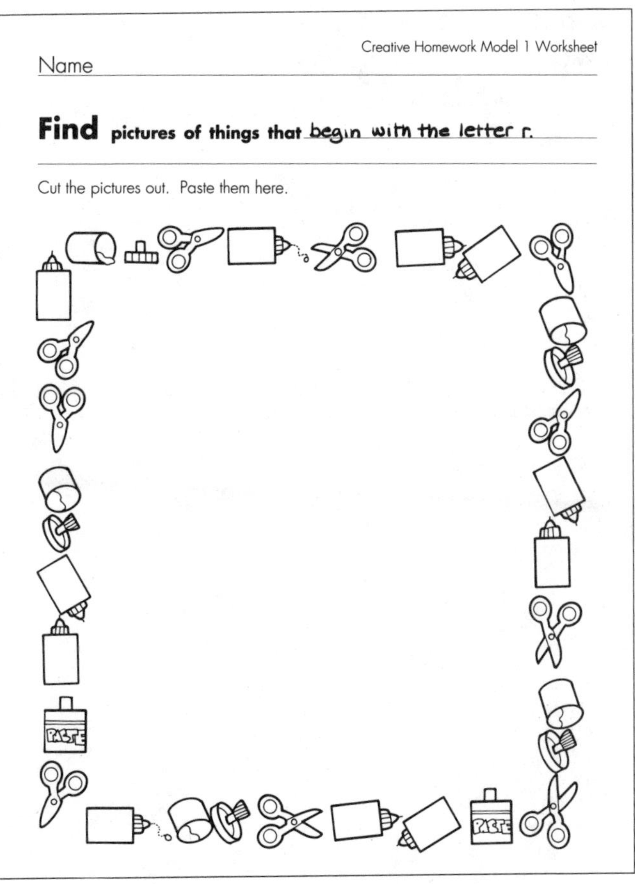

Creative Homework Model 1 Worksheet

Name

Find pictures of things that begin with the letter r.

Cut the pictures out. Paste them here.

Language Arts

Find pictures of things that:

- begin with the letter r (or any other letter).
- begin with a consonant.
- begin with a vowel.
- end with the letter g (or any other letter).
- end with a plural form.
- are green (or any other color).
- are nouns.
- are verbs.
- could be used as ideas for a story or poem.

Math

Find pictures of things that:

- represent the number 7 (or any other number).
- come in pairs.
- come by the dozen.
- are difficult to count (like ants).
- are bigger (or smaller) than 1 inch (or 2 inches, etc.).
- show a circle (or triangle, or square, etc.).

Science

Find pictures of things that:

- change colors.
- grow bigger with time.
- are living.
- are mammals.
- are insects.
- are birds.
- are reptiles.
- are plants.

Social Studies

Find pictures of things that:

- show community helpers at work.
- show kinds of transportation.
- show different kinds of jobs.
- show different kinds of homes.

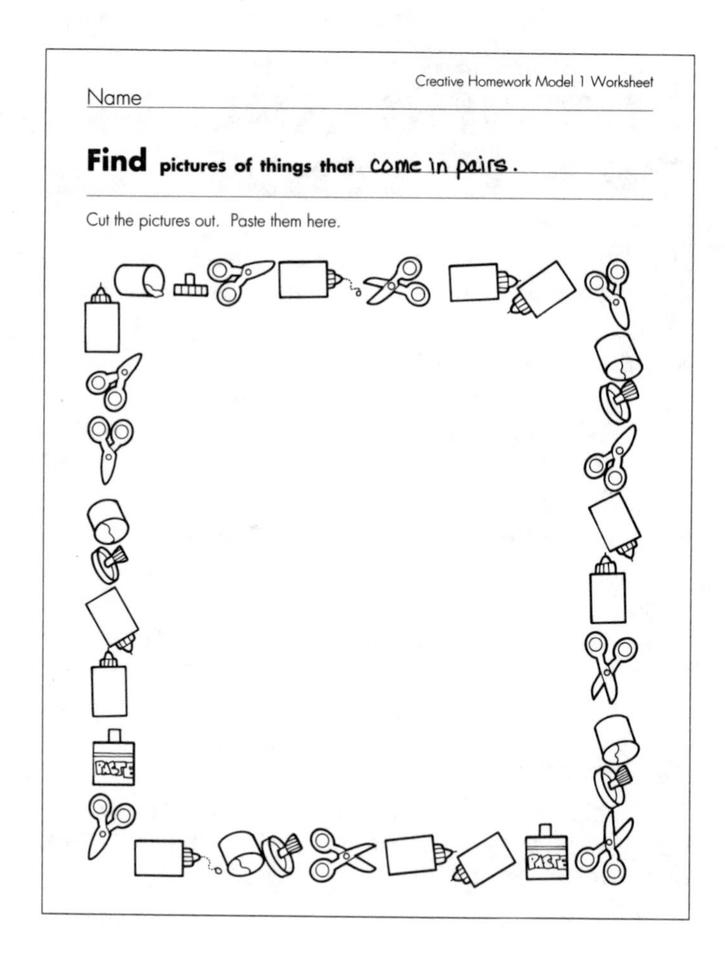

Creative Homework Model 2

SEQUENCING

This homework sheet is designed to encourage young students to draw and/or write the steps in various sequenced activities they are learning about in school.

BEFORE YOU BEGIN

Make one copy of the Creative Homework Model 2 worksheet (Appendix page 114). Write in the specific directions you want your students to follow. (See the examples below.) Circle either "Draw" or "Write." Write in the number of sequenced steps you want your students to show. Use this "master" to make a copy of the assignment for each student in your class.

EXPLAIN THE ASSIGNMENT TO STUDENTS

Talk about what it means to "draw or write steps" that show a specific activity. Ask students to tell you (for example) the steps they might follow when they plan a birthday party: 1. Buy invitations. 2. Mail the invitations. 3. Plan games. 4. Buy favors. 5. Bake a cake. 6. Decorate the house. 7. Get dressed up. 8. Have the party! If appropriate, write the steps on the board. Point out that these are the steps that show how to get ready for a birthday party. Tell students that their homework assignment will be to draw or write (specify which) the steps that show (tell asignment).

APPLICATION

This sequencing activity can be effectively used in different subject areas. You can probably think of many ways to use this homework sheet that will fit your specific curriculum needs and learning objectives. Here are some suggestions:

Language Arts

Draw or write the steps that show:

- how to get ready for school in the morning.
- how to get ready for bed at night.
- how to bake a cake.
- how to wash a dog.
- what happened in the beginning of a story, the middle of the story, and the end of the story.
- how to get a book from the library.

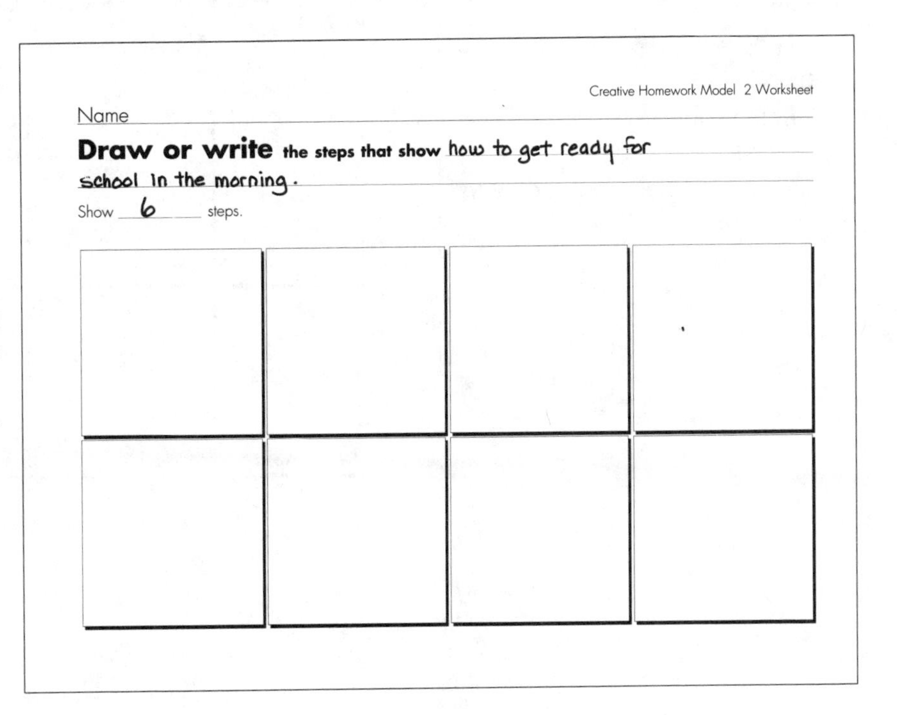

Creative Homework Model 2 Worksheet

Name

Draw or write the steps that show how to get ready for school in the morning.

Show 6 steps.

Science

Draw or write the steps that show:

- how a tadpole grows into a frog.
- how an avocado grows from a pit.
- how a caterpillar turns into a butterfly.

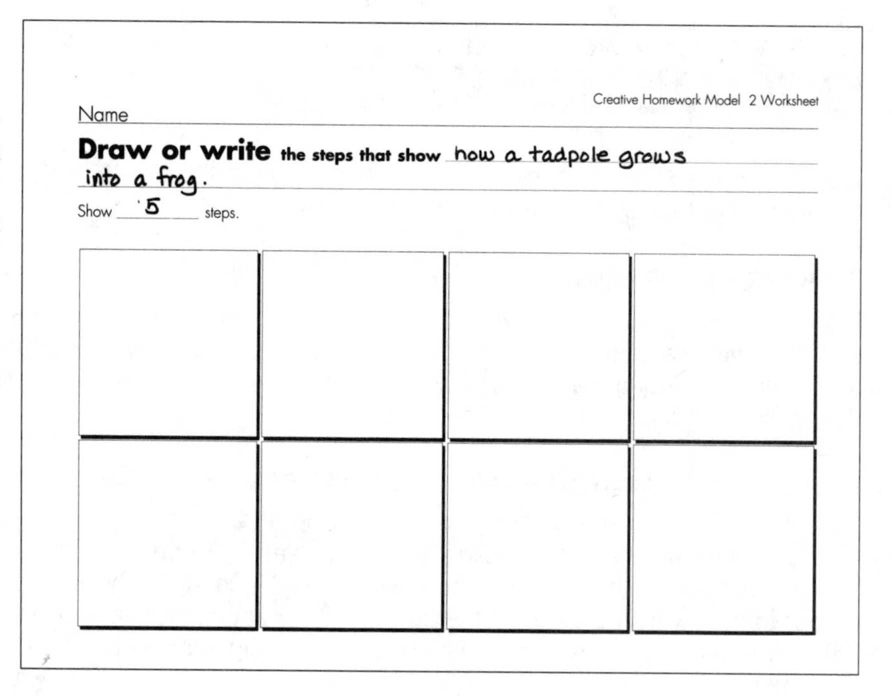

Social Studies

Draw or write the steps that show:

- how to make a salt-and-flour map.
- how to make a sugar-cube igloo.
- how mail gets from one place to another.
- how milk comes from a cow to our home.

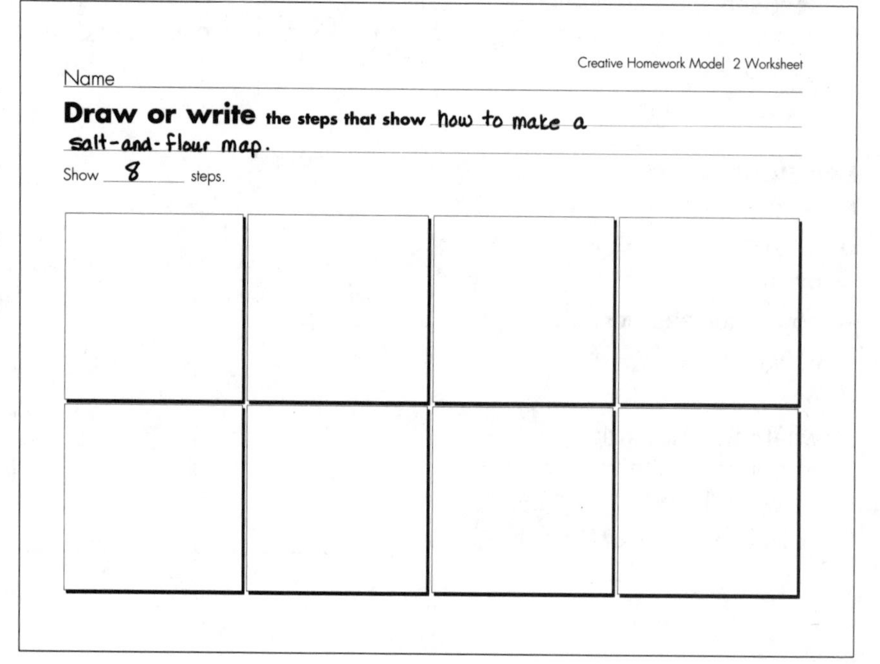

Creative Homework Model 3

CATEGORIZING AND SORTING

This homework sheet is designed to help students sort things into categories.

BEFORE YOU BEGIN

Make one copy of the Creative Homework Model 3 worksheet (Appendix page 115). Write in the specific directions you want your students to follow. (See the examples below.) Use this "master" to make a copy of the assignment for each student in your class.

Note: There are many excellent sorting activities that your students can do at home using real objects from around the house. On these assignments, ask students to have their parents help by listing what the child has sorted into each category and by signing the sheet to verify the work was done.

EXPLAIN THE ASSIGNMENT TO STUDENTS

Tell students exactly what they are to sort into (specify quantity) categories. Give some examples. Be sure to explain whether or not they will be cutting and pasting or listing objects on the worksheet. If appropriate, tell them that their parent's help—and a parent signature—will be required.

APPLICATION

This sorting activity can be effectively used in different subject areas. You can probably think of many ways to use this homework sheet that will fit your specific curriculum needs and homework learning objectives. Here are some suggestions:

Language Arts

Sort:
- a list of reading words into nouns and verbs. (Attach a list of the words to be sorted.)
- words from a (specific) story into two groups: names of people and words that tell about people.
- letters of the alphabet into consonants and vowels. (Attach a sheet of cut-out alphabet squares.)
- old buttons into any two groups you wish. Paste them on the worksheet.

Creative Homework Model 3 Worksheet

Name

Sort letters of the alphabet **into these two groups:**

1. consonants
2. vowels

Math

Sort:
- pictures from a magazine into circles and squares.
- pictures from a magazine into triangles and squares.
- numbers from 1 to 30 into even and odd.
- simple word problems into those to be solved by addition and those to be solved by subtraction. (Attach a list of the word problems.)

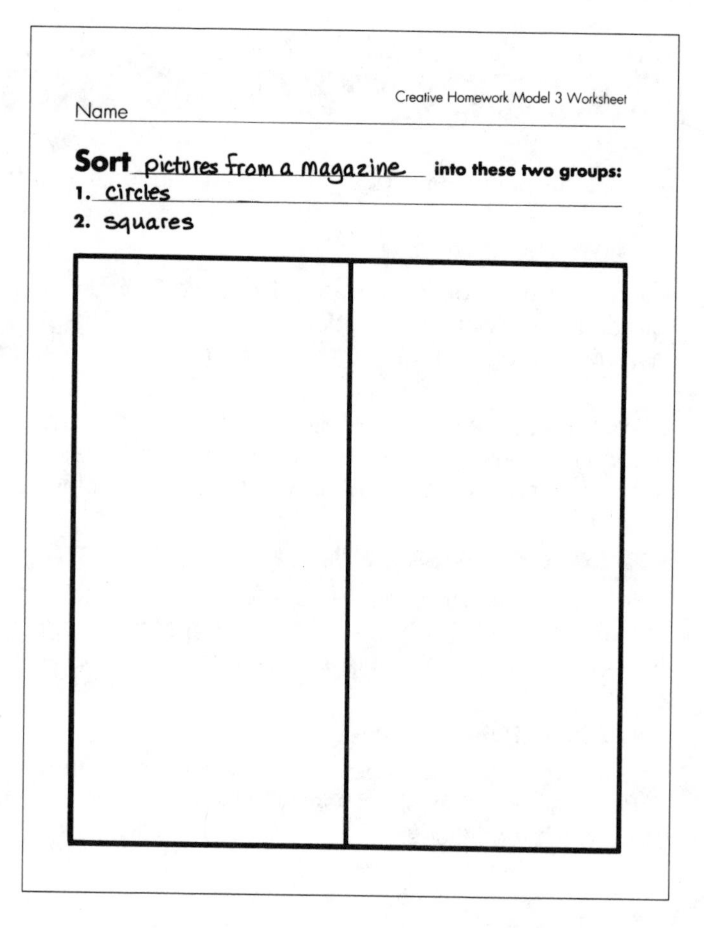

Science/Health

Sort:
- rocks in your yard into smooth and rough.
- pictures of animals into mammals and reptiles.
- pictures of animals into parents and babies.
- things in your yard that are (or were) alive and things that are not alive.
- your clothing at home into things you wear in warm weather and things you wear in cold weather.
- leaves in your yard into any two groups you wish.
- small objects at home into metal and wood.
- machines at home into those run by electricity and those run by human energy.

Social Studies

Sort:
- foods in your home into two groups: things from the dairy and things from a bakery.
- foods in your home into two groups: things that are fresh and things that are preserved.
- pictures of animals into farm and zoo groups.

Creative Homework Model 4

TELLING SOMETHING LEARNED IN YOUR OWN WORDS

This homework sheet is designed to encourage students to summarize in writing 3 things they tell someone at home about something they have learned in school.

BEFORE YOU BEGIN

Make one copy of the Creative Homework Model 4 worksheet (Appendix page 116). Write in the specific directions you want your students to follow. (See the examples below.) Use this ''master'' to make a copy of the assignment for each student in your class.

EXPLAIN THE ASSIGNMENT TO STUDENTS

Tell students that their homework assignment that night will be to tell someone at home 3 things they learned in school about (give the specific assignment). Practice a few times in class by having volunteers give examples. Show the worksheet to students. Point out that after they *tell* someone their 3 facts, they are to *write* those three things on the worksheet. Encourage students to ask their parent(s) for help in writing if necessary. Point out also that there is a space on the worksheet for their parent's signature.

APPLICATION

This activity can be effectively used in different subject areas. You can probably think of many ways to use this homework sheet that will fit your specific curriculum needs and homework learning objectives. Here are some suggestions:

Language Arts

Tell someone at home 3 things you learned about:

- when to use capital letters.
- how to use the library.
- how to write a letter.
- the characters in a story you are reading in class.

Creative Homework Model 4 Worksheet

Name

Tell **someone at home 3 things you learned today about** when to use capital letters.

Try to use full sentences. Write down what you said in the 3 spaces below. Have a parent sign this sheet.

My child told me 3 things that were learned in school today.
Parent signature

Math

Tell someone at home 3 things you learned about:
- how to do 2-digit addition (or subtraction, or multiplication, etc.).
- how to do word problems.
- how to use a ruler to measure things.

Science/Health

Tell someone at home 3 things you learned about:
- a science experiment done at school.
- what plants need to grow.
- things you should eat each day.
- the sun, the moon, or the stars.
- how animals protect themselves.
- magnets.
- how sound travels.

Social Studies

Tell someone at home 3 things you learned about:
- your community.
- your state.
- your country.
- the firefighter's job.
- the police officer's job.
- the mail carrier's job.
- sources of our clothing.
- a specific holiday.
- homes in another land.
- the globe.
- a specific famous American.

Creative Homework Model 5

USING FOUND OBJECTS TO MAKE A MODEL OF SOMETHING LEARNED

This homework sheet is designed to encourage creativity by asking students to use simple objects they find at home to make models of things they've learned about in school.

BEFORE YOU BEGIN

Make one copy of the Creative Homework Model 5 worksheet (Appendix page 117). Write in the specific directions you want your students to follow. (See the examples below.) Use this ''master'' to make a copy of the assignment for each student in your class. Pass out the worksheets.

EXPLAIN THE ASSIGNMENT TO STUDENTS

Have students look at the "found objects" border on the worksheet. Explain that "found objects" are things that can be found (for example) around the yard or in a park (like sticks, leaves, or rocks), around the house (like clothespins, empty Kleenex boxes, toilet paper rolls, Popsicle sticks), or around the neighborhood (like aluminum cans, pieces of wood, Styrofoam food containers). Ask students to give examples of other objects that might be found in their environment. Explain that their assignment will be to make something (explain the assignment) out of found objects. Point out that the worksheet has spaces for students to write down information about their project. Read the instructions together. Tell students to ask a parent for help in filling out the worksheet.

APPLICATION

This activity can be effectively used in different subject areas. You can probably think of many ways to use this sheet that will fit your curriculum needs and homework learning objectives. Here are some suggestions.

Note: Many of these assignments will require more than one night to complete. Work with students to establish deadlines. Check up on their progress at regular intervals. Because it's fun to do, this activity is a good introduction to long-range assignments for younger students.

Language Arts

Use found objects to make:

- something interesting to look at. Give it a name and write a sentence about it.
- a puppet to use in a puppet show. (Paper bags, paper plates folded in half, socks, and wooden spoons all make good puppets.)
- a diorama of a scene from a story you are reading.
- a diorama of a scene from a story you are writing.

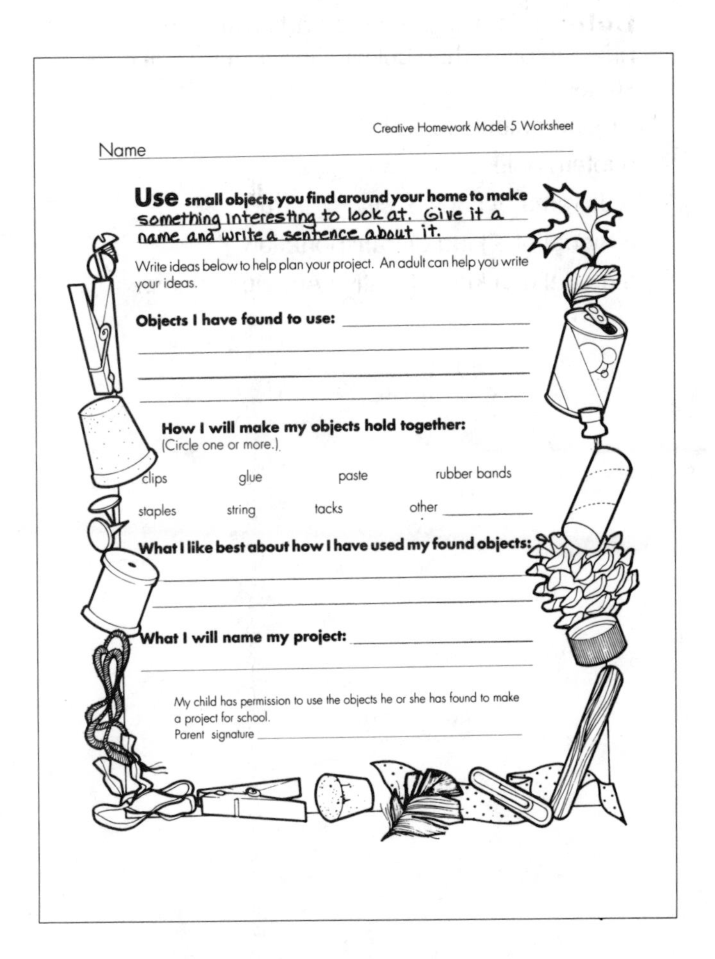

Creative Homework Model 5 Worksheet

Name ____________________

Use small objects you find around your home to make something interesting to look at. Give it a name and write a sentence about it.

Write ideas below to help plan your project. An adult can help you write your ideas.

Objects I have found to use: ____________________

How I will make my objects hold together:
(Circle one or more.)

clips glue paste rubber bands
staples string tacks other ________

What I like best about how I have used my found objects: ____________________

What I will name my project: ____________________

My child has permission to use the objects he or she has found to make a project for school.
Parent signature ____________________

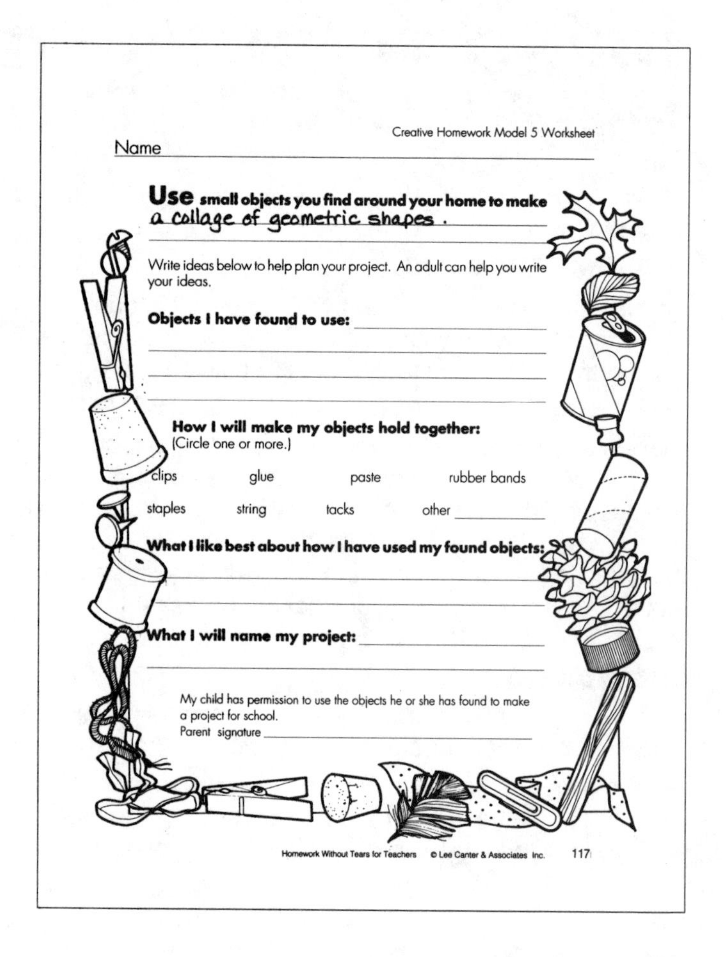

Creative Homework Model 5 Worksheet

Name ______________________

Use **small objects you find around your home to make** a collage of geometric shapes.

Write ideas below to help plan your project. An adult can help you write your ideas.

Objects I have found to use: ______________________

How I will make my objects hold together:
(Circle one or more.)

clips glue paste rubber bands

staples string tacks other ________

What I like best about how I have used my found objects:

What I will name my project: ______________________

My child has permission to use the objects he or she has found to make a project for school.
Parent signature ______________________

Homework Without Tears for Teachers © Lee Canter & Associates Inc. 117

Math

Use found objects to make:

- a collage of geometric shapes.
- the tallest structure you can that still balances!
- a structure that is 3 inches in height (or 6 inches, etc.).
- a design that shows, for example, 8 different things.
- a design that shows (for example) 2 sets of 3 things each.

Science

Use found objects to make:

- something that moves forward.
- a diorama of a forest .
- a diorama of the seashore; desert.
- a terrarium.
- a collection of man-made objects and objects found in nature.

Social Studies

Note: This assignment is particularly appropriate to give when culminating a study unit in social studies.

Use found objects to make:

- a totem pole.
- a diorama of a town, city, or farm.
- a model of a kind of transportation.
- a model of a kind of Native American home.

CONCLUSION

There is no doubt that homework can be a valuable part of the education process for all involved. It can help students develop the study skills they need to achieve better in school and develop a sense of responsibility. Homework can provide a way for parents to be productively involved in their child's education. And for you, the classroom teacher, homework can provide a valuable extension of the school day to reinforce your efforts in the classroom.

The key to making all of these benefits possible lies with you. All of the positive aspects of homework shrink to insignificance if the homework you assign is inappropriate for your students. The value of homework is relative. It is relative to the daily efforts you make to ensure that every homework assignment is meaningful and appropriate. But it is only with these efforts that you, your students and their parents can enjoy the rewards of homework completed responsibly, consistently. . . and without tears.

APPENDIX

Student Worksheets for Homework Lessons 81

Parent Tip Sheets for Homework Lessons 95

Positive Notes for Parents 103

Parent - Teacher Note 104

"How to Handle Homework Problems"
Parent Checklist 105

Creative Homework Model Worksheets 111

STUDENT WORKSHEETS FOR HOMEWORK LESSONS

Pages 83-93 of the Appendix contain the reproducible Student Worksheets that correspond to the homework lessons provided in Chapter 3, "How to Teach Your Students to Do Homework Responsibly." Each of these worksheets has been designed to both reinforce the learning objective of the lesson, and to extend that learning into the home. Keep in mind that all of these homework lessons should be presented within a two-week time period. Therefore, it would be helpful to run off copies of all the worksheets (one per student of each worksheet) before you begin teaching the homework unit.

Student Worksheets:

Student Worksheet for Lesson 2:
Returning Homework to School on Time 83

Student Worksheets for Lesson 3:
Setting Up a Study Area 84-86

Student Worksheets for Lesson 4:
Creating a Homework Survival Kit 87-88

Student Worksheets for Lesson 5:
Planning Daily Homework Time 89-90

Student Worksheet for Lesson 6:
Doing Homework on Your Own 91

Student Worksheets for Lesson 7:
Rewarding Yourself for Homework Success 92-93

Name ____

X Marks the Homework Drop Spot!

Color the X.
Put this sign at your Homework Drop Spot.

Name

Study Area Cut-Outs

Do this worksheet with a parent.

1. Choose a study area for yourself at home.
2. Color and cut out the pictures below of the things that are in your own study area.
3. Paste these pictures on your This Is My Study Area worksheet.

Name ______________________________

This Is My Study Area

Do this worksheet with a parent.

1. Paste your Study Area Cut-Outs on this sheet to show what your study area at home looks like.
2. Draw more things to make it look just like home.

DO NOT DISTURB! HOMEWORK IN PROGRESS

Name ____________________

Homework Survival Kit Cut-Outs

Do this worksheet with a parent.

1. Color all of the pictures on this page.
2. Cut out the pictures.
3. Paste the pictures on your Fill the Homework Survival Kit worksheet.

Name ____________________

Fill the Homework Survival Kit!

Do this worksheet with a parent.

1. Paste your Homework Survival Kit Cut-Outs on this page. When you are finished, your picture will show all the things that can go into a Homework Survival Kit.
2. Mark an **X** on each picture as you add it to your real Homework Survival Kit.

I agree to help my child put together a Homework Survival Kit.
Parent Signature____________________

Name ______________________________

After-School Activities Squares

Do this worksheet with a parent.

1. The pictures on this page show four things you do after school.
2. Cut out the pictures.
3. Paste them on your My Daily Schedule worksheet.

Name ____________________

My Daily Schedule

Do this worksheet with a parent.

Parent Signature ____________________

1. Look at the pictures. Read the words.
2. Think about what you do after school.
3. Paste your After-School Activities Squares in order on numbers 5, 6, 7, and 8 .

Name ______________________________

I Did It!

Do this worksheet with a parent.

Color and Cut

1. Use your favorite colors to fill in all the I's in the squares below.
2. Cut out the squares.
3. Put the squares in your Homework Survival Kit.

Paste

1. Write your name on a piece of paper. Paste an "I Did It" square on the paper and return it to school. This shows that you cut out all of the squares on your own!
2. Remember to paste an "I Did It" square on any homework you are proud of having done on your own.

I dId It	I dId It
I dId It	I dId It
I dId It	I dId It
I dId It	I dId It
I dId It	I dId It

Name ______________________________

Ways I Can Reward Myself for Doing a Good Job on Homework

1. Look carefully at all the pictures on this page. Each picture shows something that might be fun to do.
2. Cut out the pictures that show ways you would like to reward yourself for doing a good job on homework. Be sure to choose things that you really could do!
3. In the blank space, draw another way you could reward yourself.

Name ______________________________

Paste your reward squares in the surprise package below.

This is how I can reward myself for doing a good job on my homework!

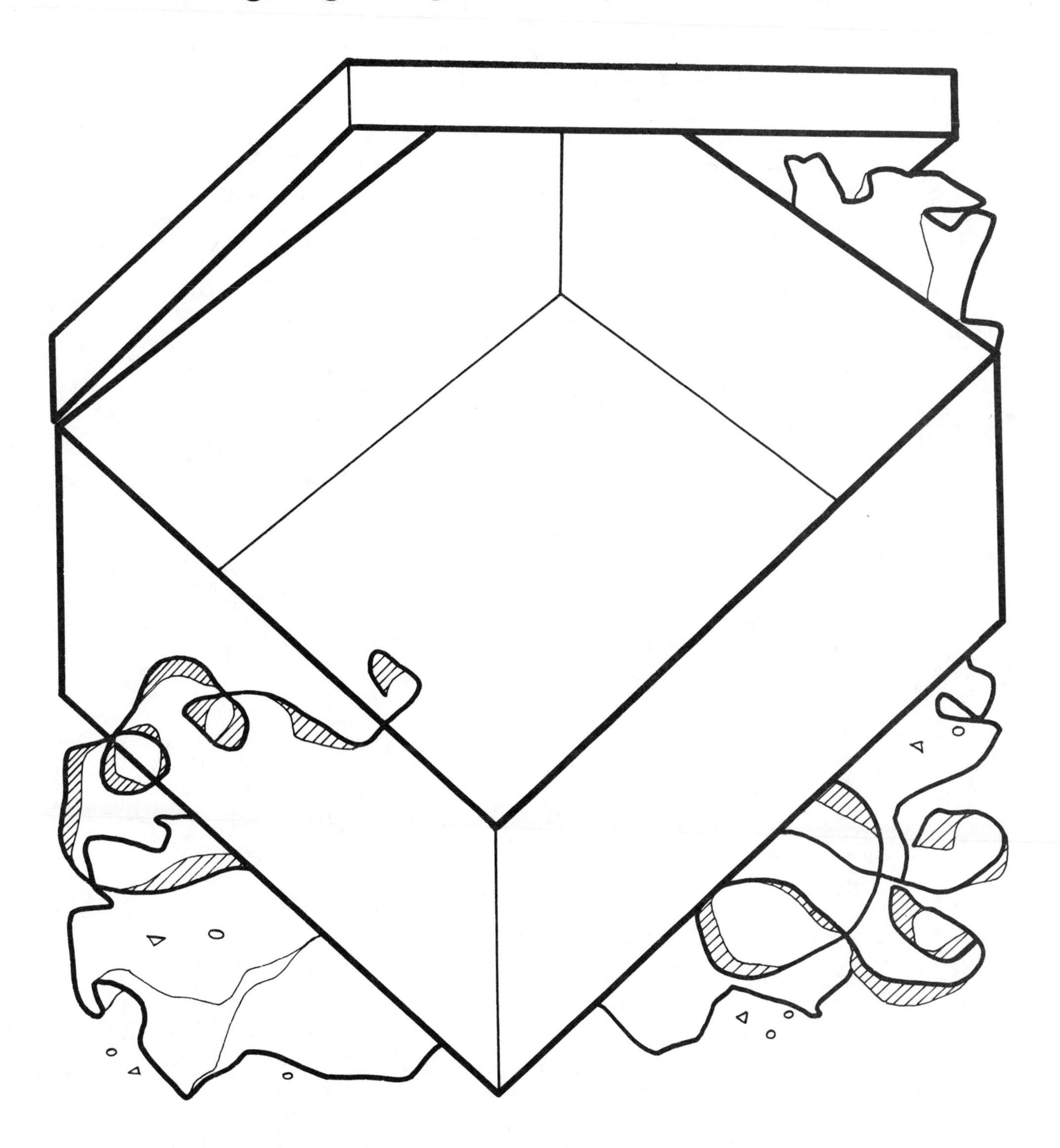

PARENT TIP SHEETS FOR HOMEWORK LESSONS

Pages 97-102 of the Appendix contain the reproducible Parent Tip Sheets that correspond to the homework lessons provided in Chapter 3, "How to Teach Your Students to Do Homework Responsibly." Each of these Parent Tip Sheets has been designed to give parents the information they need to encourage their children to deal more successfully with homework. Keep in mind that all of the homework lessons should be presented within a two-week time period. Therefore, it would be helpful to run off copies of all the Parent Tip Sheets (one per student of each sheet) before you begin teaching the homework unit.

Parent Tip Sheets:

(Note: There is no Parent Tip Sheet for Lesson 1.)

Parent Tip Sheet for Lesson 2:
Returning Homework to School on Time 97

Parent Tip Sheet for Lesson 3:
Setting Up a Study Area 98

Parent Tip Sheet for Lesson 4:
Creating a Homework Survival Kit 99

Parent Tip Sheet for Lesson 5:
Planning Daily Homework Time 100

Parent Tip Sheet for Lesson 6:
Doing Homework on Your Own 101

Parent Tip Sheet for Lesson 7:
Rewarding Yourself for Homework Success 102

Parent Tip Sheet 2

CHOOSE A HOMEWORK DROP SPOT

In the early grades, your child must begin to develop the study habits that will be the foundation of his or her success in school in the years to come. Remembering to bring homework assignments back to school is one of the most important habits your child must develop.

Choosing a special Homework Drop Spot at home will help your child develop the habit of always putting completed assignments in the same place each night.

PRAISE your child each time completed homework is put in the Homework Drop Spot.

Agree on the Homework Drop Spot your child chooses. Make sure it is in a location that is convenient for you, too.

Help your child choose a Homework Drop Spot that's easy to "spot" on the way out the door in the morning.

Respect the Homework Drop Spot. Don't let other things clutter or cover it.

Parent Tip Sheet 3

CHOOSE A STUDY AREA AT HOME

HOMEWORK **WITH** TEARS

To do homework successfully, your child must have a place in which to work. The study area must be well lit, quiet, and have all necessary supplies.

Keep the radio and TV off while homework is being done.

Whenever possible, keep the study area off limits to brothers and sisters during homework time.

PRAISE your child when he or she does homework in the study area.

HOMEWORK **WITHOUT** TEARS

Help your child choose a location at home in which homework will be done. Even if your child does most of the homework at another location after school, there still should be a place in the home in which he or she can study.

Remember that your child does not need a lot of space in which to do homework. The kitchen table or a corner of the living room is fine, as long as it is well lit and quiet during homework time.

Parent Tip Sheet 4

CREATE A HOMEWORK SURVIVAL KIT

HOMEWORK **WITH** TEARS

One of the keys to getting homework done is having supplies in one place. A Homework Survival Kit—containing supplies needed to do homework—will prevent your child from being continually distracted by the need to go searching for supplies, and will free you from last-minute trips to the store for paper, tape, glue, etc.

If your child does homework at a location other than home (such as the library or an after-school care program) make sure that his or her homework supplies are available there.

Respect your child's Homework Survival Kit. Don't use these supplies for other family needs.

AGREE with your child that it is his or her responsibility to remind you when any of the Homework Survival Kit materials are getting low and need replacing.

Give Homework Survival Kit materials as gifts. A dictionary, for example, is a special present that a child will use over and over again.

These are the supplies needed for a Homework Survival Kit:

*pencils • *writing paper • *crayons
markers • ruler • sharpener
erasers • glue or paste • tape
construction paper • stapler
scissors • paper clips • children's dictionary

* These are the most important supplies your child needs. Try to obtain these items as soon as possible. Add additional homework supplies as you are able to.

You don't need to gather all the materials in one day, but don't wait too long. Your child needs these supplies to do his or her best job on homework.

HOMEWORK **WITHOUT** TEARS

Parent Tip Sheet 5

SCHEDULE DAILY HOMEWORK TIME

Help your child develop good homework habits by encouraging him or her to start homework at the same time each day. By scheduling Daily Homework Time, you will not only help your child get work done on time, but you will also ensure that homework is done at a time when you are available to assist your child.

Post your child's completed My Daily Schedule cut-and-paste activity on the refrigerator.

It is your responsibility to schedule Daily Homework Time for your child. For young children, the best time is often as soon as they (and you) arrive home at the end of the day.

Encourage your child to do homework during Daily Homework Time by giving lots of **PRAISE** each time homework is done appropriately.

Remind your child each day when he or she is to do homework.

Select a time when you or another responsible adult will be available to assist your child.

Try to schedule the same Daily Homework Time for all of your children. (This will make it more convenient for you to be available.)

HOMEWORK
WITHOUT
TEARS

Parent Tip Sheet 6

CHILDREN MUST WORK ON THEIR OWN

HOMEWORK **WITH** TEARS

Homework teaches children responsibility. Through homework, children learn skills they must develop if they are to grow to be independent, motivated and successful adults: how to follow directions, how to begin and complete a task, and how to manage time. By encouraging your child to work on his or her own, you are helping develop these important life skills.

Check to see that your child is doing homework at the proper time.

PRAISE your child when he or she does homework independently. Let your child know just how proud you really are!

Suggest that your child call a friend if he or she needs help.

Give your child help only if he or she makes a real effort to do the work first.

HOMEWORK **WITHOUT** TEARS

Parent Tip Sheet 7

MOTIVATE CHILDREN WITH PRAISE

Children need encouragement and support from the people whose opinions they value the most—their parents. Your consistent praise can encourage your child to feel good about his or her ability *and* motivate your child to do his or her best work.

Each night praise your child about some specific accomplishment. Say something positive about a specific goal your child has set. Example: "I really like how you're doing your homework on your own now."

It is important to **PRAISE** all homework efforts. Let your child know just how proud you are of how hard he or she is working.

Use Super Praise to motivate your child!

First, one parent praises the child: "I really appreciate how hard you're working to do your homework. You finished it all during Daily Homework Time and you did a great job. I want to make sure Dad hears about this when he gets home."

Second, this parent praises the child in front of the other parent: "Patty did a really fine job on her homework today. She started it without complaining, she stayed with it, and she did a super job on it."

Finally, the other parent praises the child: "I really feel proud of you, getting such a good report from Mom. You're really doing fine!"

If you're a single parent, you can use a grandparent, a neighbor , or a family friend as your partner in delivering Super Praise. Any adult whose approval your child will value can fill the role of the second person offering praise.

HOMEWORK **WITHOUT** TEARS

Positive Notes for Parents

Run off copies of these notes and keep them handy for use throughout the year.

HOMEWORK SUPERSTAR!

Dear ____________________,

Thought you'd like to know

that ____________________

is doing a great job on

homework because

____

____

____

____

Signed

____

Date

Parent-Teacher Note

Run off copies of this form and keep them handy for use throughout the year.

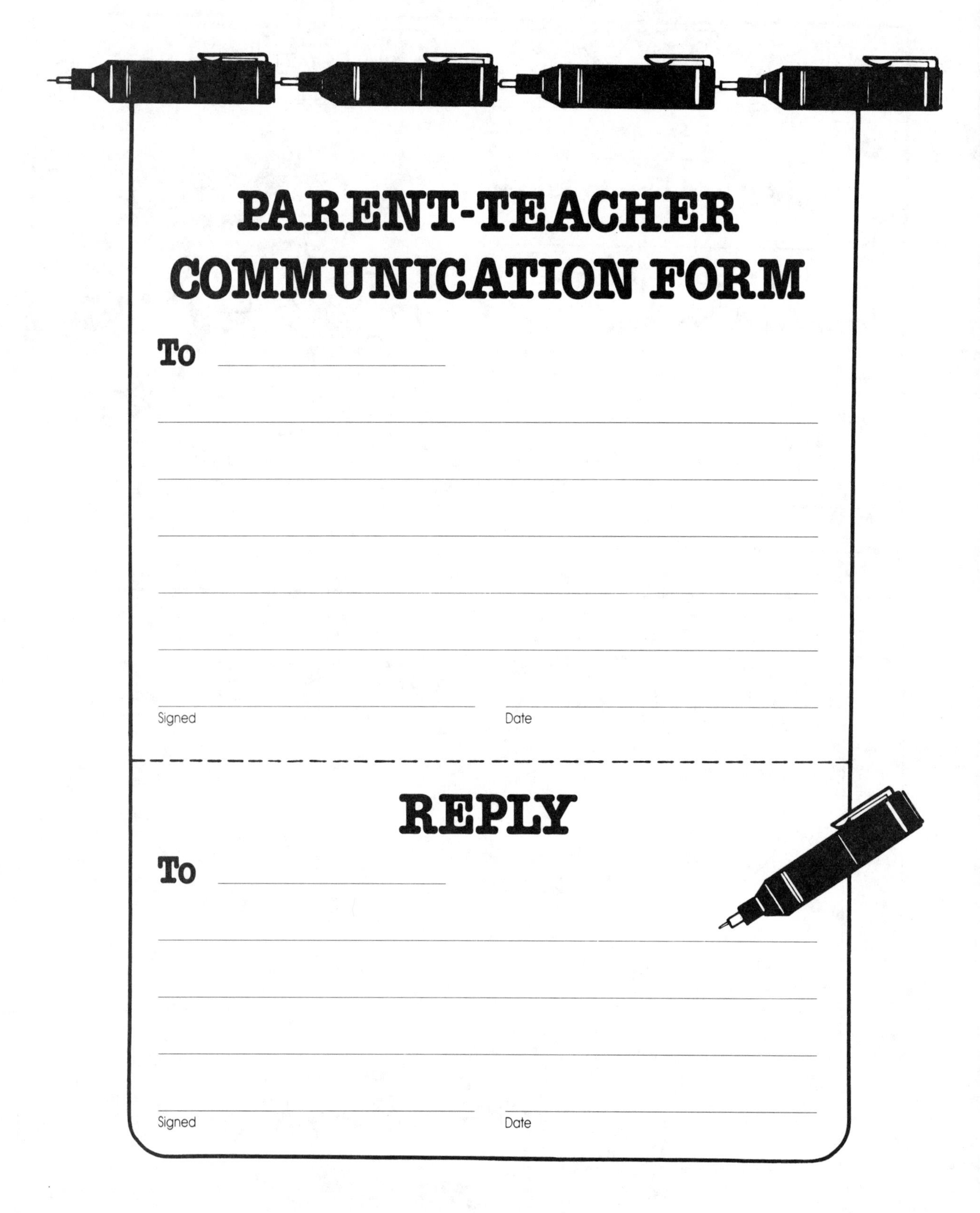

PARENT-TEACHER COMMUNICATION FORM

To ____________________

____

____

____

____

____

Signed ____________________ Date ____________________

- -

REPLY

To ____________________

____

____

____

Signed ____________________ Date ____________________

HOW TO HANDLE HOMEWORK PROBLEMS

Parent Checklist

Pages 107-110 of the Appendix contain the reproducible "How to Handle Homework Problems" parent checklist. This checklist has been designed to help you help parents deal with the most common homework problems:

What to do when children will not do their best work.

What to do when children refuse to do homework.

What to do when children fail to bring assignments home.

What to do when children take all night to finish homework.

What to do when children will not do homework on their own.

What to do when children will not do homework if parents are not home.

Suggestions for using the parent checklist can be found on pages 61 and 62.

Note: You are welcome to translate these pages into any language appropriate for your parents.

For the parent(s) of________________________________

How to Handle Homework Problems

Doing homework assignments appropriately is an important responsibility that young children must develop. If your child is having difficulty getting homework done you must step in and help solve the problem. Keep in mind that the development of poor study habits at an early age can cause problems later. The following checklist can help you isolate your child's homework problem--and find the solution.

1 Review your actions.

yes no

☐ ☐ Have you established homework as a priority for your child?

☐ ☐ Have you set up a quiet study area at home for your child?

☐ ☐ Have you encouraged your child to do homework during a pre-planned daily homework time?

☐ ☐ Have you praised your child when homework is done appropriately?

☐ ☐ Have you given your child appropriate help when needed (such as reading the directions together to make sure the child understands what he or she is to do)?

If you answered "yes" to the above questions and your child is still having a problem with homework, you must take additional steps. To begin, determine precisely what the problem is.

2 Pinpoint the problem.

Check the box that best describes your situation.

☐ **A** My child does not do his or her best work on homework assignments. The work is often sloppy or incomplete.

☐ **B** My child refuses to do homework.

☐ **C** My child does not bring assignments home.

☐ **D** My child takes all night to finish homework.

☐ **E** My child will not do homework on his or her own.

☐ **F** My child will not do homework if parents are not home.

☐ **G** Other ________________________________

Now check the corresponding response in the following section.

3 Tell your child exactly what you expect.

It is important to state clearly and specifically what actions you expect of your child regarding homework.

☐ **A** "I've been looking at your homework assignments and I know you can do a better job. You are not to rush through your assignments. I want you to take your time and do the best work you can. Sloppy work with a lot of mistakes is not acceptable."

☐ **B** "I expect you to do all of your homework every night. It is your responsibility, and I know you can do it."

☐ **C** "I expect you to bring home all your assigned work, and all the books you need to complete your assignments. If you finish your homework during free time at school, I expect you to bring it home so that I can see it."

Note: Ask the teacher to have your child write down each day's homework assignments. The list is checked and signed by the teacher and brought home by your child. When your child completes the assignments, you sign the list and have your child return it to the teacher.

☐ **D** "I expect you to get all of your homework done during Daily Homework Time. We have set aside plenty of time. You cannot take all evening to complete your work."

Note: Your child may take too much time to do homework because he or she is working in a distracting environment. Make sure that during Daily Homework Time your child has no access to TV, stereo, or other distractions and is not disturbed by brothers and sisters.

☐ **E** "I expect you to do your homework without my help. I will not sit with you or do your work for you. I know you can do it on your own."

☐ **F** "I expect you to get your homework done every night whether or not I am home."

Note: Make sure that the person responsible for your child's care knows where your child is expected to do homework (in the study area), when homework is to be done (during Daily Homework Time—which should be posted) and how your child is to do it (on his or her own). It is a good idea to sit down with your child and the caregiver and communicate your expectation that homework will be done just as though you were home.

In addition, it is helpful to telephone your child at the beginning of Daily Homework Time to be sure homework has begun. Call back, if possible, at the end of Daily Homework Time to make sure your child has completed his or her assignments. Have your child leave completed homework out for you to check when you get home. You may phase out this monitoring as your child begins to work responsibly.

☐ **G** Other ______________________________

____

4 Praise your child whenever expectations are met.

Praising your child for good work is the best way to encourage continued best efforts. In giving praise, it is important to be specific. Let your child know exactly what you are praising him or her for.

☐ **A** "This homework paper is very neat. It shows me that you are taking your time on your homework assignments. Thanks for the great effort!"

☐ **B** "I really like the way you've been so responsible about getting your homework done. You're doing a terrific job!"

☐ **C** "It's great to see that you remembered to bring home all of your homework."

☐ **D** "Good job! I'm pleased to see that you got your homework done on time. I'm so proud of you!"

☐ **E** "I'm really proud of the way you are doing all of this work on your own. I knew you could!"

☐ **F** "You have been doing such a terrific job on your homework when I'm not here. Keep up the good work!"

☐ **G** Other ______________________________

____

5 Provide additional incentives.

Special incentives may be necessary at first to get your child into the habit of doing homework appropriately. Here are some ideas:

☐ **Homework Contract**: Draw up a Homework Contract between you and your child. A Homework Contract is an effective motivator that can work well with children of any age. It is an especially valuable tool because it encourages children to accept responsibility for an agreement made between them and their parents. The Homework Contract is appropriate for dealing with any homework problem.

A Homework Contract states:

- **How homework will be done.**

  For example:

  Homework must be completed each night.

  Homework assignments must be brought home from school.

  Homework must be done whether or not the parent is home.

- **The number of points earned each time homework is done appropriately.**
- **The reward the child will receive when a certain number of points is earned.**

For example, a child might receive one point each night homework is completed. When five points are reached, a reward is earned. The younger the child, the more quickly he or she should be able to earn the reward. For children in grades 1-3, a suggested duration for the contract is three to five days.

☐ **Beat the Clock**: "Beat the Clock" is particularly helpful with children who seem to take all night to do their homework. First, determine how long it should take for your child to finish homework. (If you are not sure, contact the teacher.) Then, at the start of Daily Homework Time, tell your child that you have a new, fun way to help him or her get through homework:

1. "You'll have an hour (or half hour, or whatever time you determine) to get tonight's assignment finished."
2. "I'm going to set this oven timer (stopwatch, clock radio, etc.) for 60 minutes. If you get your homework done correctly before the timer goes off, then you'll get . . .(whatever reward you've chosen)."

As your child begins "beating the clock" on a regular basis, replace the rewards with stickers. When your child has accumulated five stickers, he or she gets a reward or prize.

Phasing Out: The number of stickers needed to earn a reward should increase as the child becomes more responsible about doing homework.

☐ **Chunking**: "Chunking" is a great technique to use when your child complains that his or her homework assignments are just too much to handle. For example, your child might look at an assignment of 24 math problems, and feel overwhelmed. "Chunking" can make the job seem manageable. "Chunking" means dividing a big assignment into smaller chunks. For example, a 24-problem math assignment could be broken into six groups of four problems each. When your child finishes each group of four problems, he or she earns a small reward.

Tell your child: "This is a big homework assignment, but I know that you can do it all! Let's play a game that will make it easier. I've marked off the first four problems on your worksheet. I want you to do these problems on your own. When you've finished them, you will receive a prize! We'll keep working this way with every group of four problems until the whole assignment is done!"

Phasing Out: As your child becomes more comfortable with long assignments, break them down into fewer chunks (3 groups of 8 problems each, then 2 groups of 12 problems each).

6 Back up your words with action.

If the preceding steps do not succeed in getting your child to do homework appropriately, you must take a stand. You must let your child know that his or her behavior will result in a loss of privileges. Tell your child: "You can choose either to do your homework as we have discussed, or you will lose these privileges: (For example) You may not go outside to play. You will not watch TV. You will not be allowed to listen to music. You will not be allowed to use the telephone to either make or receive calls." And then stick to these demands. You must make it very clear to your child that homework is a responsibility that must be taken seriously.

7 If problems persist, contact the teacher.

If your child continues to not complete homework appropriately, discuss with the teacher the possibility of imposing loss of privileges at school. Loss of recess or after-school detention lets your child know that you and the school are working together to ensure that he or she behaves responsibly.

Additional comments: ______________________________

____

____

____

____

Teacher's Signature______________________________

CREATIVE HOMEWORK MODEL WORKSHEETS

Pages 113-117 of the Appendix contain the reproducible worksheets for the Creative Homework Models presented in Chapter 7. Make one copy of each worksheet per student prior to giving the lesson.

Creative Homework Model Worksheets:

Creative Homework Model 1 Worksheet:
FIND pictures of things that _____ 113

Creative Homework Model 2 Worksheet:
DRAW or WRITE the steps that show _____ 114

Creative Homework Model 3 Worksheet:
SORT_____into these two groups: 115

Creative Homework Model 4 Worksheet:
TELL someone at home about 3 things you learned today 116

Creative Homework Model 5 Worksheet:
USE small objects you find around your home to make_____ 117

Name ______________________________

Find **pictures of things that** ______________________________

____

Cut the pictures out. Paste them here.

Name ______________________________

Draw or write **the steps that show** ______________________________

____

Show ________ steps.

Name ______________________________

Sort ______________________ **into these two groups:**

1. ______________________________

2. ______________________________

Name ____

Tell someone at home 3 things you learned today about ______________________________

Try to use full sentences. Write down what you said in the 3 spaces below. Have a parent sign this sheet.

My child told me 3 things that were learned in school today.
Parent signature ______________________________

Name ____

Use small objects you find around your home to make

____

____

Write ideas below to help plan your project. An adult can help you write your ideas.

Objects I have found to use: ____________________

____

____

____

How I will make my objects hold together:
(Circle one or more.)

clips glue paste rubber bands

staples string tacks other ____________

What I like best about how I have used my found objects:

____

____

What I will name my project: ____________________

____

My child has permission to use the objects he or she has found to make a project for school.

Parent signature ________________________________

RECOMMENDED READING

For readers desiring more information about homework, the following works are recommended for the subject areas listed below.

ACADEMIC ACHIEVEMENT

Fredrick, W.C., & Walberg, H.J. (1980). Learning as a function of time. *Journal of Educational Research, 73,* 183-204.

Keith, T. (1986). *Homework.* West Lafayette, IN.: Kappa Delta Pi.

Lavin, D.E. (1965). *The prediction of academic performance.* New York: Russell Sage Foundation.

EFFECTIVENESS AT THE ELEMENTARY SCHOOL LEVEL

Doane, B.S. (1973). The effects of homework and locus-of-control on arithmetic skills achievement in fourth-grade students. *Dissertation Abstracts International, 33,* 5548A.

Harnischfeger, A. (1980). Curricular control and learning time: District policy, teacher strategy, and pupil choice. *Educational Evaluation and Policy Analysis, 2 (6),* 19-30.

Hudson, J.A. (1966). A pilot study of the influence of homework in seventh grade mathematics and attitudes toward homework in the Fayetteville public schools. *Dissertation Abstracts International, 26,* 906.

Koch, E.A. (1965). Homework in arithmetic. *The Arithmetic Teacher, 12,* 9-13.

Levine,V. & Worley, W.R. (1985, April). *The impact of television and homework time on cognitive and noncognitive outcomes.* Paper presented at the annual meeting of the American Educational Research Association, Chicago.

Maertens, N., & Johnston J. (1972). Effects of arithmetic homework upon the attitude and achievement of fourth, fifth, and sixth grade pupils. *School Science and Mathematics, 72,* 117-126.

Paschal, R.A., Weinstein, T., & Walberg, H.J. (1984). The effects of homework on learning: A quantitative synthesis. *Journal of Educational Research, 78,* 97-104.

Stanley, J.C. (1980). Manipulate important educational variables. *Educational Psychologist,* 15, 164-171.

Wolf, R.M. (1979). Achievement in the United States. In H.J. Walberg (Ed.), *Educational environments and effects: Evaluation, policy, productivity.* Berkeley, CA.: McCutchan.

EFFECTIVENESS FOR HIGH AND LOW ACHIEVERS

Keith, T.Z. (1982). Time spent on homework and high school grades: A large-sample path analysis. *Journal of Educational Psychology, 74,* 248-253.

Stanley, op. cit.

GRADED VERSUS NON-GRADED

Paschal, et. al., op. cit.

AS A MEANS TO INDIVIDUALIZE INSTRUCTION

Bradley, R.M. (1967). An experimental study of individualized versus blanket-type homework assignments in elementary school mathematics. *Dissertation Abstracts International, 28,* 3874a.

Check, J.F., (1966). Homework: Is It needed? *The Clearing House,* 41, 143-147.

QUALITY VERSUS QUANTITY

Leonard, M.H. (1965). An experimental study of homework at the intermediate-grade level. *Dissertation Abstracts International, 26,* 3782.

PARENTAL INVOLVEMENT

Epstein, J.L. (1984, April). *Effects of teacher practices of parent involvement for change in student achievement in reading and math.* Paper presented at the annual meeting of the American Educational Research Association, New Orleans.

LaConte, R.T. (1981). *Homework as a learning experience.* Washington, D.C.: National Education Association.

Maertens & Johnston, op. cit.

Walberg, H.J. (1984). Improving the productivity of America's schools. *Educational Leadership, 41 (8),* 19-30.

HOMEWORK POLICIES

Keith, op. cit.

RESPONSIBILITY

Fiesen, C.D. (1978). *The results of surveys, questionnaires, and polls regarding homework.* Iowa City, IA.: University of Iowa.

Keith and Page, op. cit.

ADDITIONAL SUPPORT FOR YOUR HOMEWORK PROGRAM

HOMEWORK WITHOUT TEARS® BOOKS

Homework Without Tears - A Parent's Guide for Motivating Children to Do Homework and to Succeed in School
Co-authored by Lee Hausner, Ph.D.
A practical book that educators can use to help parents end the nightly battle over homework. Parents learn how to take an active role in the homework process. **#CA1205 $7.95**

Homework Without Tears for Teachers, Grades 4-6
Teachers will use this comprehensive guide to teach their students how to do homework. Contains homework policy guidelines, complete lesson plans, reproducible homework models and parent tip sheets.
#CA1212 $9.95

Homework Organizer for Students
This delightfully written and illustrated book helps students remember their assignments, organize their time, develop good study habits and track their progress. Recommended for grades 4-8.
#CA1223 $3.95

Homework Motivators
These clever reinforcers will encourage students to do their very best on all homework assignments. Includes bulletin board ideas, individual incentives, charts and awards. Recommended for grades 1-6.
#CA1225 $6.95

Creative Homework
Teachers can quickly create interesting and educational homework assignments that allow students to apply the skills they've learned that day. Reproducible models includes suggestions for use in many subject areas.

Grades 1-3	**#CA1231**	**$5.95**
Grades 4-6	**#CA1232**	**$5.95**

Order from your local school supply dealer.

HOMEWORK WITHOUT TEARS® WORKSHOP FOR PARENTS

One of Lee Canter's associates can travel to your school or district to conduct a 2 1/2-hour workshop. Parents will understand what their role is in the homework process and learn techniques to influence their children toward more productive study habits.

For more information on conducting a Homework Without Tears Workshop for Parents, call Lee Canter & Associates at (800)262-4347. In California, call (213)395-3221